Kevin **Ley**

Furniture
Workshop

A Woodworker's Guide

GUILD OF MASTER CRAFTSMAN PUBLICATIONS

This collection first published 2004 by
Guild of Master Craftsman Publications Ltd
Castle Place, 166 High Street,
Lewes, East Sussex BN7 1XU

ISBN 1 86108 375 0

Cover photography by Kevin Ley
Principal illustrations by Ian Hall and Simon Rodway

Publisher: Paul Richardson
Art Director: Ian Smith
Production Manager: Stuart Poole
Managing Editor: Gerrie Purcell
Commissioning Editor: April McCroskie
Editor: Olivia Underhill
Designer: Jo Patterson

Colour origination by CTT Reproduction, London
Printed and bound by Kyodo Printing, Singapore

Furniture

Workshop

A Woodworker's Guide

Contents

NOTES

Though every effort has been made to ensure that the information in this book was accurate at the time of writing, it is inevitable that specifications and availability of some of the products mentioned will change from time to time. Readers are therefore urged to contact manufacturers or suppliers for up-to-date information before ordering. A comprehensive selection of contact details can be found on pages 122-123.

MEASUREMENTS

Although care has been taken to ensure that the measurements in this book are true and accurate, the metric measurements are only conversions from imperial; they have been rounded up or down to the nearest millimetre. When following the projects, use either the imperial or metric; do not mix units. Detailed conversion tables are provided on pages 120-121.

FOREWORD

Kevin first appeared in *Furniture and Cabinetmaking* magazine in Issue Two when he was introduced to the readers in a feature. By Issue Five he was writing for us. He has been writing almost non-stop since then. I have known Kevin for quite a few years now – since my very first involvement with the magazine – before I was Editor. His furniture is straightforward, clean-lined, and very approachable. No one would feel intimidated by Kevin's furniture – it is to be used and lived with. It has honesty and no pretensions, people feel comfortable with it. This is its appeal, he lets the wood do most of the talking.

Eventually, when I met the man behind the furniture, I found that many of the things that appeal about the furniture also apply to the man. Like his furniture he is easy to get on with. While Kevin takes his making very seriously, he has a tremendous sense of the pleasure of life and that extends into his furniture making – he thoroughly enjoys the whole process.

Being creative in any field, once you have the inspiration, usually involves a series of activities that have to happen chronologically. Kevin is very pragmatic about his furniture-making methods and is extremely organised. He has to be, partly because his workshop, like many people's, is not that big. Obviously his former life in the RAF has something to do with this, but that is his natural inclination, too. One of his great adages is 'KISS', or as Kevin describes it 'Keep It Simple Soldier', and this is very much his approach. This is why I think woodworkers will like Kevin's philosophy. Self taught, his method and making is achievable, practical and down-to-earth. It is based on no-nonsense reality, but that does not mean that you can't enjoy it too! Keen woodies everywhere will enjoy this book – so get stuck in and enjoy!

Colin Eden-Eadon

Colin Eden-Eadon
Editor, *Furniture and Cabinetmaking*

INTRODUCTION

I spend many hours in my workshop and do all I can to make them very happy hours.

I was once told by my field craft instructor that any fool can be uncomfortable – a good soldier takes the trouble not to be. As a soldier this enables you to operate more effectively for longer, and as a maker the same applies. The Shakers said that 'Beauty rests on utility' and nowhere does this apply more than in the workshop. To me a beautiful workshop is light, warm, dry, clean, safe, and well-equipped with necessary tools. I could also mis-quote William Morris: 'Have nothing in your workshop that you do not know to be useful or believe to be necessary'. Enough of the quotes already – just make sure that you take the trouble to make your working environment as comfortable, effective, and safe as possible!

No workshop is ever big enough, certainly in mine any piece of equipment has to justify the space it occupies. Careful pre-planning and sequencing is necessary for large projects, but it is amazing what can be achieved when you work at it. Make sure all available space is used – a shelf above that window, storage in the roof space, under or behind the bench.

I try not to keep wood in stock. It takes up space and represents dead money. As a maker of custom pieces I don't know what I will be making the next piece out of, so I let the timber merchants store it for me. I just make sure I know who has, or is likely to have, what and where. Stocks are bought in, allowing plenty of time for the wood to condition, either in my workshop or timber store, both of which are heated and dehumidified.

I find networking with other makers is enjoyable and useful – most are happy to share details and experiences, and offer advice or encouragement, and any I give is always returned – in spades. Some though, are shortsighted and secretive - frightened of losing business or having their ideas stolen or copied. I am proud if anyone wants to copy my work and if they can find a client – good luck to them. As to stealing ideas or designs – there is little new under the sun! I take my influences and ideas from all sorts of places, often not really knowing the source. It is what I do – put my interpretation on my client's wishes, based on my memory bank of ideas – wherever they came from.

I am a great believer in labour-saving power tools and machinery. They take the drudgery out and leave the time to be spent on adding real individuality and quality. A machine can thickness a board far quicker and better than I can by hand, but it can't choose that particular piece of figured wood to be book-matched into the door panels, and make a stunning feature. Many of the original Arts and Crafts Movement makers failed because they took hand making too far – they just priced themselves out of the market. Maximizing appropriate use of machinery and power tools keeps us cost effective.

I always select each piece of my timber before I buy it and am prepared, if necessary, to pay extra for the privilege. I am careful to cultivate my timber merchants and observe the etiquette of the yard. Go by appointment to select, keep out of the way, be safety aware, and always restack any boards you have gone through. If you play by the rules you will be welcome, and usually helped.

In the making of a piece nothing is more important than the initial choice of the pieces of timber and then the specific allocation to areas of the final piece. The decisions about which part of each board goes where on the piece of furniture can be a long process but I do not resent the time taken – it always pays off.

The first part of this book is about my workshop and the tools I use. I hope it demonstrates that I do not have anything beyond the range of most serious makers, amateur or professional, in terms of space or equipment. There is a list of useful suppliers of tools, equipment and materials on pages 122 (UK) and 123 (USA). The second part is about some of the projects I have made in it. I hope it is of help and encouragement to existing or potential makers and they have as much pleasure and satisfaction as I do in the setting up and the making.

Kevin Ley

Workshop
Set-up

& Tools

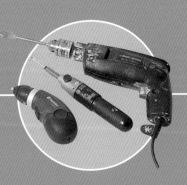

Part one Part one Par

- What is your aim?
- Can you make enough pieces to achieve this?
- How much time can you allocate?
- Are you self-disciplined enough to be self-employed?
- Can you afford the necessary tools and equipment?
- Can you deal with all aspects of the business?

House buyers may see this as a garage – but it's an excellent workshop!

I thoroughly enjoyed the 'Face and Edge' series of articles by Paul Richardson in *Furniture and Cabinetmaking* magazine. They must have been good – I agreed with just about everything he said! Though when I tried to apply some of his principles to writing articles, it didn't seem to work quite as he indicated…

I was commissioned into the RAF Regiment at the age of 18, so when I changed career at the age of 44, I only knew one way to go about it – to the music of a brass band!

I had been trained to approach problems or tactical situations in a particular way, using certain broad principles. They had served me well in a range of circumstances throughout my RAF Regiment career and I used them to set up my business, they are recounted here, in case they are of interest or use to anyone else.

start up

○ TAKE AIM

Selecting and maintaining your aim is the key principle. I thought long and hard about it – if I got this wrong I knew all would be lost. If you don't define clearly what you want to achieve you can't possibly achieve it, or even know whether or not you have. Once I had decided on my aim, all my efforts were directed towards achieving it.

Ask yourself – do you want to become a millionaire, owning a number of busy workshops, doing large-batch production for retail outlets, or do you want to make small craft items for sale at fairs or markets, to supplement your pension? I could go on with an infinite number of options and still not cover yours – only you can do that.

My aim was: **'To achieve a reasonable income by making bespoke furniture, as a self-employed sole trader.'** This aim posed three questions:

Light, dry and warm – a good place for the wood, work, equipment and maker

① WHAT IS A REASONABLE INCOME?

I made a very careful assessment of assets and liabilities, arriving at the annual income required to achieve my desired life style. The overall figure was broken down to an hourly workshop rate to be charged. When calculating this rate I allowed for non-productive time for administration, sickness, training, research, holidays and unforeseen contingencies.

② CAN I MAKE AND SELL SUFFICIENT BESPOKE FURNITURE TO ACHIEVE IT?

Once I decided I wanted to go in this direction I began to time how long it took me to make my hobby pieces for our home, and the orders I got from friends. I compared the sort of item I had made with something similar, commercially produced, and noted the cost, I attributed this value to the piece I had made, and worked backwards to establish the hourly rate I was earning. Of course a one-off, individual

item would have a premium, but one must start somewhere, and I started to get a feel for the sort of income possible.

It quickly became apparent that the premium was essential – I could not compete with mass-produced items. The large retailers, such as IKEA and the like, provide very high value for money in their range of items. If you really want a fright, look at some of the pine, bare-sanded pieces exported from Eastern Europe. You couldn't buy the materials for the price of these finished items!

③ DO I HAVE THE SKILLS AND ATTRIBUTES TO BE A SELF-EMPLOYED SOLE TRADER?

This means more than 'not having a boss' – it is having the self-discipline and ability to be the boss, as well as the workforce. Did I want to work on my own – with little or no social exchange or contact? Was I able to keep tabs on all the various aspects of the business as well as make the product? Would I sweep the floor as well as take the client to lunch? In addition, could I sell what I made as well as making what I sold?

Once I had answered these questions to my own satisfaction I judged that I had defined an achievable aim and set about achieving it.

The nine-drawer apothecary chest that suited a client's budget

○ MANPOWER AND MATERIALS

It's essential to know your strengths and weaknesses so you can maximize the former and minimize the latter. I am not a skilled turner, so I found someone who was and subcontracted any major work to him. I did the same in other areas, such as carving and marquetry.

Assess the tools you need – I am a great believer in not buying something 'just in case you need it'. It's much better to buy it when you actually need it. I often find that the necessity of having to go and get a new tool, mothers the invention of finding another way to get the same result, thus removing the need and expense. When I do buy machines or hand tools I assess the very best I can afford and buy the next one up!

Hiring or renting time on occasional-use items can be very cost effective, I know a maker who hires a pad and belt sander by the hour in a local production workshop.

It is fundamental that the workshop must be a pleasant place for me, my work, wood, and tools – warm, dry, and light, at least. As well as working space I find a clean office and/or design area essential.

‘I like to think that the workshop is still working for me while I'm off having a good time! It is very pleasing to come in on a Monday morning and strip every clamp I have off a major piece, because they have been working all weekend while the glue sets’

⬤ ECONOMY OF EFFORT

I work out a sequence of events for making that gives me best use of machine settings and repeat cuts. 'Dead' time – overnight and weekends – is used for drying, setting, and curing. I like to think that the workshop is still working for me while I'm off having a good time! It is very pleasing to come in on a Monday morning and strip every clamp I have off a major piece, because they have all been working all weekend while the glue set.

Remember the 80/20 rule which states that 80% of any given task is usually achieved with 20% of the effort. I know this might offend the philosophy of some, but consider – one client wanted a 14-drawer apothecary's chest, but blanched at the price – so I offered a nine-drawer version which was within budget, and everyone was happy!

A secret dovetail in a mitre is a great piece of craftsmanship – but might a biscuit be an acceptable option at a fraction of the cost?

Biscuit-reinforced mitres
instead of secret dovetails
bring prices down

The turned legs of this ash chest
of drawers were subcontracted out

'As well as making
what you sell, you
must sell what
you make'

Your aim

Operation

- Do I have a back-up plan if something goes wrong?
- How can I get affordable advertizing?
- What makes my work stand out from the competition?
- How can I stay focused and maintain morale?
- How important is administration to my business?

Free publicity is good advertizing.
Try to get the glossies interested in you!

The previous section covered the ways in which I fixed my aim, sorted out manpower and materials and worked out efficient ways to save time, effort – and of course money!

◯ LINES OF SUPPLY

If I rely on someone else for any aspect of my operation, I make sure I have an alternative. This could apply to timber supplies, spares for machines or delivery of my product – make sure no one can hold you to ransom! I hold a number of simple consumable machine spares, such as drive belts and carbon brushes for motors and telephone contacts who can supply anything else within 24 hours. You only discover a machine is not working when you need it. I have two of some essential machines such as sanders and routers.

start up

Walnut bureau – this over-the-top piece kept Kevin busy in a lean time, achieved lots of free publicity and became a wedding gift for Yvonne

Speculative pieces displayed in a local museum

◯ PROPAGANDA

'I know I waste half the money I spend on advertizing – but I don't know which half' (Henry Ford).

One of the best ways of avoiding wasting money on advertizing is not to pay for it at all! If you can think of anything interesting to say about yourself, or something you have made, it may be newsworthy for a local newspaper or even a national glossy. It is just a matter of fulfilling their requirements while achieving your own.

Once I found out (by asking) what sort of photos they wanted, I found it was easy to get shots of my work, and my phone number, into the monthly glossies. I also found out that I got very few orders as a direct result but that clients from other sources were very impressed that my work had been featured.

I let the local Arts Advisor in the education department, and my local museum know I had speculative pieces available for display in any exhibitions, and was included in several as a 'local artist'.

One of the best outlets I found was to approach local building societies, and offer to brighten up their boring window display with some of my work. People who use building societies are home owners or savers – or in other words my potential clients.

Not having a showroom I used our cottage, and over the years completely furnished it with my own pieces. Our eclectic tastes enabled me to have a variety of woods and styles, I was also able to display and sell speculative pieces, which I made during time 'resting' between commissions.

One 'over the top' piece was a bureau with 22 drawers and 12 secret compartments. This got me into all the local papers and on the regional TV news, even a display in a local department store with a competition to find the secret compartments.

I recently bought an up-market, high performance sports car. The manufacturer has a high quality magazine sent free to owners, circulation 250,000, twice a year. A couple of phone calls and they will be doing a feature on my work soon. Their customer base is also mine – that's targeted free advertizing – be an opportunist!

INTELLIGENCE

Know your enemy – I checked the local competition to see what I could do better. I saw what service was offered, checked his product, looked at his prices. I found a fitted kitchen maker who didn't do free-standing individual pieces – just like I didn't do fitted kitchens – we agreed to pass on suitable clients.

TRAINING

I had not had the luxury of formal training in the art and skills required but felt that I could acquire them, because I loved doing it. Training need not be formal, it can come from magazines, videos, short informal weekend courses, and on the job. I trained to the level I required to achieve my immediate aim and found that the necessary skills came with practice.

APPRECIATE THE SITUATION

Don't fight a battle you can't win. Some times it isn't the order you don't get that breaks you, but the one you do. I was approached by a very well known retail outlet in London to make original pieces for them (as a result of photos in the 'glossies') but to do it I would have to cut my prices too far – anyone can be a busy fool.

I have also had clients with whom I felt no rapport, or I felt were too demanding or unreasonable, and I was usually right – they rarely got better. Now I cut my losses early.

SECURITY

All major assets: me, my tools, workshop, display pieces, and work in progress, are protected. Applicable arrangements are made for insurance, physical security, fire, first aid and medical matters.

Sycamore and fumed oak desk. The company logo was subcontracted to a specialist marquetry firm

MAINTENANCE OF MORALE

I maintain my morale by making my work and working conditions as good as I can, and by having a really nice delivery van! Now, I make sure to take time off, having found that accidents and mistakes happen when I am working too long/late/hard and my concentration goes. When giving a delivery date I always give myself more time than I think I need – no client has ever complained about something finished early.

Recognizing I am a service industry I enjoy working for my clients and do my very best to ensure they enjoy the whole experience of buying bespoke furniture from me – then they come back.

Writing articles and books is an interesting and stimulating diversion which, though it could hardly be described as a 'rest', certainly provides a welcome change.

ADMINISTRATION

Time spent on administration and organization could be regarded as non-productive, but not getting it right can be even more counter-productive. I have a system and stick to it, and one morning a week is set aside for paperwork.

After using an accountant for a couple of years I found that if I kept the books and attended to the paperwork carefully, the end-of-year accounts only took me a short time, and saved me a good deal of money. They take even less time now, as I have programmed my computer to do running accounts, which give me a clear picture of the state of the business finances at all times. I think it is very difficult to run a business properly if you don't understand the finances – just throwing it all in a box and handing it over to the accountant at the end of the year is too risky.

This 'delivery van' helps maintain morale!

THE WILL TO WIN

If you want something badly enough you can make it happen. Making a living from furniture-making has not been easy – nothing worthwhile ever is. It has taken a lot of effort and concentration, but I have loved, and am loving, every minute!

Your aim

Workshop principles

All my workshops have had a previous life – a ham smoking house, an apple store, a cow byre, a dairy, the uninhabited rooms in the farmhouse we were converting, and numerous garages. I made plenty of mistakes and learned many lessons from their conversions. In this section I will show how I applied this experience to my present home, above the double garage next to our cottage.

Fed up with freezing his vital statistics in a motley succession of draughty garages and outbuildings, Kevin suggests ways to turn your frozen assets into hot profits

BASIC CONSTRUCTION

The first huge advantage of this prospective workshop was that there could be no question of it being shared with a car. Cars don't like wood dust, and wood and tools do not like the moisture a wet car brings in.

I looked at the basic size and construction of the empty garage before we bought the house next to it. My intended workshop area was a room on the first floor but the ceiling sloped down into the room, so the floor space and headroom were tight.

The entrance door was wide and there were stone steps on the outside plus an easy straight run up seven wooden stairs inside. I could get my kit in, but was there enough room and would the floor take the weight?

An old garage workshop

Try to avoid situations like this – it's not much good in the winter!

FLOOR

There was a good size RSJ (Rolled Steel Joist) under the middle of the floor and another under the end over the garage doors. The floor joists did not have noggins between them so I added these, to improve the rigidity. The floorboards were fairly even but with worn, rough surfaces and gaps between. In a previous workshop I had covered the uneven concrete floor with T&G chipboard (tongue and groove), spot-glued down and levelled with No-Nails glue. This surface was warmer, kinder to dropped edge tools and falling makers and easier to move machines and work over – well worth it.

I decided that just covering this floor with hardboard would give a smooth, flat surface and stop dust raining down and draughts coming up. I misted the 8 x 4ft (2440 x 1220mm) sheets of hardboard with water on each side, stacked them, covered them with a tarpaulin and left them outside for a couple of hours to dampen and swell slightly. Then I fixed them at 6in (150mm) centres using a hired, heavy-duty staple gun. As the hardboard covering dried, it shrank to a tight fit, with no 'bubbles'.

FLOOR SPACE

It was immediately apparent that the floor space would need careful planning, especially as my first order was a batch of four partners' desks. This concentrated my mind wonderfully. The sloping ceiling restricted headroom, but I could use the loft and the garages below for more storage. I planned to store general DIY and decorating stuff, house and garden tools in the garages below, and wood and cut timber for future projects in the loft above.

You can save a lot of workshop space by installing the dust extractor outside, in another building or a waterproof cupboard. Here it would fit easily in the garage, between the cars, with the trunking running under the workshop floor. Added advantages are gravity-assisted removal of chips and dust, noise reduction, and the shortest possible run to its main customers – the planer and table saw.

The floor space would be adequate with the cast-iron planer and table saw placed centrally over the RSJ, with 9ft 6in (2740mm) clearance either side, and the radial arm saw between the main benches on the east gable end.

I rarely use timber boards more than 15ft (4575mm) long. Now I could cut boards to length on the radial arm saw before processing them further on the other machines. This was a real luxury – in previous workshops I have had to pass long pieces through doors and windows to the machines, and sometimes do the initial cutting out elsewhere with a chainsaw!

FLOOR PLAN AND MAIN FEATURES

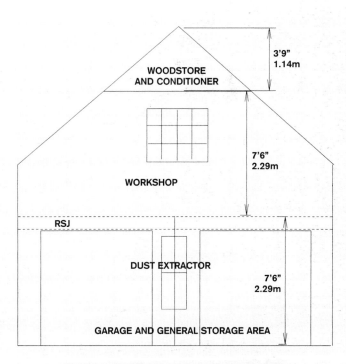

CROSS SECTION AND MAIN FEATURES

Warm and comfortable,
light and airy

The eaves offer a good
storage space for timber

TIMBER DELIVERY

Most of my timber comes straight off the lorry through the central window between the benches. I remove the opening casement and lay carpet on the sill to slide it over. The last load was 35 cubic feet of 1⅛in zebrano (*Microberlinia brazzavillensis*) in 10ft x up to 3ft-wide boards – quite a lift, but better than carrying it round to the side door and manoeuvring it up the stairs, around and over the machines and into the workshop!

WALLS AND CEILINGS

The most important thing I have learned in this business is that tools, wood, and furniture-makers need to be warm, dry and – the tools at least – lightly oiled!

The walls were single-skin 4in (100mm) concrete block, so I decided to line them with insulated plasterboard. This has an aluminium foil vapour barrier and 2in (50mm) thick polystyrene insulation pre-bonded to the back. It comes in 8 x 4ft boards and you can cut it to size with a knife or saw. I used my jigsaw and glued it to the concrete wall with a special bonding plaster.

Internal insulation is ideal for an intermittently heated building as it is closest to the heat source, and warms up quickly as you are not heating the external walls. This method is particularly ideal for concrete, stone, block, or brick buildings.

If you have a wooden building, you can line it on the inside with a polythene sheet for a vapour barrier, lay glass fibre or rock wool between battens, then fix plasterboard over the battens to provide a fire barrier and a suitable surface for painting.

LOFT

I cut a hole in the plasterboard ceiling of my workshop to confirm it was a traditional cut roof construction, rather than trusses which would have restricted the available space. All was as expected and the rafters and joists were good and strong. The purlins between the gable ends and supporting the centre of the rafters seemed a little light for their span so I bolted another piece of timber of the same dimension to each, to beef them up. This would help support the extra weight of the timber I planned to store up there.

For loft access I cut through one of the ceiling joists, supporting the ends on noggins between the adjacent joists, and made a large trap door.

I laid wires for the loft lights and power, and for the workshop below, leaving the tails out to connect up later. I also installed my big old hi-fi speakers on the loft floor with just the front grilles visible through framed holes cut in the ceiling over the benches, saving more space!

To insulate the ceiling, including the sloped part, I laid 4in (100mm) of glass fibre between the joists and rafters. The existing ceiling plasterboard already had a foil vapour barrier and heat reflector backing. Next I boarded the floor of the loft with T&G chipboard to spread the load and make sliding wood about easier. When I had fitted the lights, I sealed the overlap of the roofing felt with gaffer tape, to make it airtight, in order for me to install a dehumidifier.

TIMBER STOCKS

I do not store a lot of wood, preferring to buy it as needed. I use a lot of different timbers and it would not make economic or storage sense to keep large stocks on site. Where possible, I cut wood for future projects and stick

Kevin's Top Tips

○ **Anyone can be cold, damp and uncomfortable but a good craftsman makes his working conditions as good as he can.**

○ **Tools and makers should be clean, dry and only slightly oiled!**

○ **If you are not comfortable in your workshop, neither is your work, material or equipment.**

and stack them in this store or the workshop to condition for as long as possible before I dimension them. If I kept more wood in the loft I'd have to consider the extra weight.

LIGHT

Some ten years ago I noticed that it was more difficult to see the finer divisions on my engineer's rule. My optician tried to sell me a pair of glasses to help me focus close up. I was having none of it. A monocle would do nicely – at half the price! He also said that bright lights assist with close work as the lens in the eye is using a smaller aperture that gives a greater depth of field.

Two windows give a fair amount of daylight but I needed brighter light on the work. I fixed a pair of 5ft (1525mm) strip-lights over the benches, another pair over the planer and table saw, and another pair over the lathe and sharpening bench. I fixed pairs of adjustable tungsten spotlights over each bench, the bandsaw and the lathe, all on individual switches.

POWER AND HEAT

I had a ring main installed around the workshop with plenty of double or quadruple sockets, up high so that portable tool cables would not be in the way, and installed permanent cables under the floor, over the ceiling, or be-hind the purlins. The planer and table saw were on a separate power circuit. Everything electrical was connected to a consumer unit with circuit breakers and an earth trip-switch. I did some of the manual work myself and got an electrician to finish it and check everything for safety and insurance purposes.

Now I needed some heat. I installed a sawdust burner in the workshop, with a surplus electric storage heater from the house as backup. However, in the five years I have used the workshop I have not needed the storage heater.

DÉCOR AND STORAGE

At this stage I taped over the joins on the plasterboard lining, filled the cracks and holes and gave the whole place two coats of white paint to brighten it up. Then I moved everything in.

I installed racks for frequently used hand tools and clamps. I keep most of my kit covered in a variety of containers – drawers under work surfaces, cupboards and even apple boxes keep things tidy and accessible.

MAINTENANCE

An untidy workshop is a dangerous, inefficient place. My RAF training makes it second nature to keep everything clean, tidy, and properly stowed. I believe this is also essential in a small workshop. Once a year I stop production and have a clean up. Ruthlessly I sentence offcuts to the wood-burner, clean out nooks and crannies, vacuum the walls and give everything a coat of paint. Hmm – just like the annual inspections I cursed in a previous existence!

OVERVIEW

This workshop is too small, but workshops always are. It is, however, warm, dry, light, secure and convenient, pleasant and healthy to work in and my best yet. When I took photos of the inside, 35 cubic feet of zebrano for a boardroom table and eight chairs had just been delivered. It had been cut out, initially dimensioned, and stacked in the workshop to condition. As you can see there is still room to work, though a bit of magic may be required for the latter stages of the 6ft (1830mm) diameter octagonal table!

Though I am happy with this workshop, one day I would like to build one in wood from scratch and include all those little extras – a gallery area, a nice desk, a rest room and bar, a hot tub, sauna...!

Workshop safety

Health and safety should be our first consideration and second nature in our craft. I try to emphasize safety specifics in context, but the aim of this section is to cover the general field and offer some food for thought. Safety isn't glamourous, but making your operation safer might save your life – and at least you'll be able to buy your round!

I wish I could order a whole round!

If you can still order five pints with one hand, count yourself lucky! Kevin takes a wry look at health and safety in the workshop

GENERAL

Most of us work alone, so make sure you have a plan for assistance. If I am injured my wife, Yvonne, may be first on the scene, so she knows all the arrangements and what action to take.

I tried to imagine everything that could go wrong – fire, electric shock, minor and major injury, health problems, break-ins, etc. I decided what I would need to do, and with what, to tackle the situation. Then I worked out what I could do to prevent disasters happening in the first place!

GOOD HOUSEKEEPING

I keep the work area clean, tidy, and uncluttered. I label cans, replace lids and caps immediately to reduce spillage, and remove rubbish, particularly oily rags, regularly. Off-cuts go straight into racks or the firewood box.

I hook electric leads and hoses up out of the way. I clean the windows and lights and sweep up nails and screws that may cause injury or damage work, as well as vacuuming.

ELECTRICS

Though I did some of the wiring myself, it was tested and inspected by a qualified electrician, for safety and insurance purposes. When we moved here I tested the Residual Current Detector (RCD), which turns the electricity off if

See no evil, hear no evil! Safety gear – ear defenders and goggles

Electrical – isolation switch, RCD,
labelled circuit breakers, notice

First-aid box – note the useful contact
numbers for the doctor, hospital, neighbour

there is a fault. Interestingly it had been fitted to the wall but not connected to the circuit, so was completely useless! The electricity company wanted a small fortune to wire it up in three weeks' time, but my friendly village electrician did it on the spot, and tested it, for a very reasonable fee! On his advice I added a more sensitive RCD in the workshop, so the existing one became the backup.

I laid permanent cables out of harm's way and I inspect portable power cables regularly. All circuits are correctly fused, circuit breakers are labelled and electrical faults are dealt with immediately.

The fuse box, with its isolation switch cutting all power to the workshop, is clearly labelled and a notice on the entrance door indicates where it is. I switch the power off whenever I leave the workshop.

FIRE

I am very aware that a wood workshop is a fire waiting to happen, so prevention is uppermost in my mind. No smoking is allowed, and the sawdust burner is separated from flammable material by a stone and brick surround.

Machine motors get hot after a long session, so I never leave shavings or dust near them. I also go back in to the workshop a couple of hours after I have finished to make sure everything has cooled down.

I keep a pressurized-water fire extinguisher, suitable for organic fuelled fires, near the stove. Near the benches, I keep a BCF extinguisher, suitable for all fires, including electrical. The garden hose is close to the entrance and connected up and a bucket of sand is also available for spills or to smother a small fire. A heat sensor alarm in the workshop is connected to the house alarm.

I discovered when researching this topic that the BCF extinguisher is now obsolete, being considered a threat to the ozone layer, and should be replaced with a CO_2 type.

A workshop fire can build up quickly, so getting out of my first-floor workshop could be a problem. The stairs offer the only real way out. The window at the far end is too small for a quick exit, but I leave a rope there in case. I plan to use the BCF fire extinguisher to knock down any fire and exit down the stairs. The main thing is that I have thought about it and planned to get to the exit side of the fire quickly. I will attack the fire from the safe side.

When I use solvents I ensure the workshop is well ventilated so there is no build-up of fumes. I reduce the risk of dust explosions by using extractors and filters, but if dust becomes a hazard, spark and fire sources are reduced and the shop ventilated. I take particular care when loading the stove with dusty waste.

HEALTH

Experience has taught me that if I'm unwell, the best thing to do is rest, sleep, eat properly and recover. Get well, then get working. Now that I'm my own boss, I can do this without guilt, knowing I will bounce back far quicker. Illness, injury, tiredness, medication or alcohol reduce concentration, increase the hazard in an already dangerous environment and make mistakes more likely.

A clean, warm, dry, well-lit and ventilated workplace is also important to health, comfort and productivity. I use goggles, ear-defenders, dust face masks, heavy work gloves, light latex gloves and a full-face protective helmet with filtered air over the face for really dusty work, such as

Fire extinguishers – pressurized water, BCF and sand bucket. Note – BCF is now obsolete and should be replaced with CO2

Safety gear – helmet, ear defenders, dust mask, goggles, work gloves, light latex gloves

turning or routing. I attach a dust extractor to machines, but it's hard to remove dust from lathes and routers efficiently. I use an air filter that cleans and re-circulates workshop air to eliminate dust that escapes the extractor.

Though many finishes are water-based, many other solvents have an adverse effect on the respiratory system, eyes and skin, and cause light-headedness. I read and follow the instructions on the container, wear gloves, goggles, and ventilate the workshop – or use them outside if possible. Masks and filters are no good for fumes – only dust.

LIFTING AND CARRYING

The greatest modern cause of back problems is putting shopping in the back of a hatchback car, apparently. You hold the heavy load at arms' length, with back bent. It's just like putting a long board over a planer or table saw. I use roller stands to support long work, make sure of my footing and lift with back straight and arms and legs bent.

LEARNING THE HARD WAY

I will cover safety measures for specific machines and tools in future articles. Common sense, risk assessment and minimization are the keys. On some occasions I did not use them!

Early on in my woodworking I stabbed my left palm when de-barking a small piece of wood with a blunt chisel in one hand, holding the work down with the other. Cost – six stitches, time off and work slowed. Lessons learned – sharp cutting tools are easier to control, work should be properly anchored, and you should keep behind the cutting edge of hand tools.

I was bitten by a bandsaw in the right hand when making repetitive cuts to produce small blocks, at the end of a long day. Cost – ten stitches, work stopped for several days and project delivered late – plus loss of face at GMC Publications! Lessons learned – use push sticks, concentrate, do not place hands within 4in of powered blades, and don't tell your editor why the article is late!

I absentmindedly placed a 2ft metal rule on the in-feed table of my planer. It was a similar colour to the table and I didn't notice it when I later planed a board. I fed the rule into the machine under the board and there was a loud bang as it flew past me and embedded itself into the wall. Cost – a change of underwear. Lessons learned – keep machine tables clear, and – my life-long rule – never stand in the line of fire! I'm sure everyone has such war stories and each minor injury or scare serves as a warning.

FIRST AID

I keep a first-aid kit in my workshop with an assortment of bandages, dressings and antiseptic. I don't want to bleed on the work! If you do cut off an important bit, wrap it in a bag of frozen peas – they may be able to stitch it back on. It is much more tedious having a new bit made from your spare tissue in other areas – take it from one who 'nose'!

I have eye-wash fluid, an eye bath and a mirror in case I get something in my eye. I am already first-aid trained, but most likely to be the casualty. My wife, who's likely to be first on the scene, has also been trained, and we've discussed emergency actions. First-aid training for at least one family member is highly desirable and usually available in your local area. Inside the door of my first-aid cabinet are emergency telephone numbers for the doctor, local hospital, a neighbour and my wife at work.

Kevin's Top Tips

○ Think ahead!

○ Imagine what could go wrong: fire, electric shock, minor or major injury, break in, and so on.

○ Plan your immediate action and ensure the kit required is available.

○ Then try to work out how to prevent it happening in the first place!

Fire with fire-proof surround and 9in kerb

Fire alarm sensor head and Microclene filter

Dust extractor and trunking

● SECURITY

Our cottage is isolated so I asked the local crime prevention officer for security advice and followed it. All approaches to the house are covered by automatic security lights, which I find useful if I have to go out and about after dark.

We had several NACOSS-approved security companies offer systems and quotes and chose a monitored fire-and-security alarm system, which includes the garage and workshop. I felt that the contents of the workshop and garage were at the same risk of fire and theft as those in the house – or even higher.

I have fitted proper security locks to all doors and windows, and the whole system is operated every night and whenever we're out. When will house alarms be as easy to set as cars?

● INSURANCE

The alarm system reduced the insurance premium. Shop around for home/business insurance, insuring the tools, workshop and business on the same policy, if possible, to avoid territorial disputes in the event of a claim. I also have separate accident insurance for personal injury. Health, sickness and income protection policies are also available from a good broker.

● MIND YOUR 'P'S

I hope this article has got you thinking. Ours is a potentially dangerous game, injuries can be severe and we should be aware of the risks and avoid them. Make use of advice from your local police, fire service, and first-aid training centre. Remember – Proper Practice, Preparation, and Planning, Promotes Personal Protection, and Produces Perfect Projects – boom-boom!

Crafty with handtools

Like many self-taught people, some of my initial purchases were toys rather than tools and their limitations quickly became apparent. After wasting time and money I finally arrived at my present set of hand tools.

When I see the inside of some workshops with racks of saws, planes and chisels, I sometimes wonder what they are there for. I only want what is needed to make furniture – I don't need ornaments!

There is no 'correct' set of hand tools, we all have our own ways of measuring and marking, holding, clamping, hitting, cutting, chopping, scraping, and flattening our raw material when shaping it into a fine piece of furniture.

In this section I recall some of my good and bad buys, so you can avoid some of my blunders and share my successes.

You always need more hand tools with rosewood handles . . . Right? Wrong! Get crafty and save some cash

● GUIDING PRINCIPLES

You must establish in your own mind whether you are a maker or a collector. Are you buying beautifully made tools because you need them – or as a present to yourself? A plane cuts no better with a rosewood handle, but it is nice to look at.

Initially poverty forced me into the 'make do and mend' mentality of tool purchase, then a mixture of enthusiasm and anxiety made me rush into trying to buy everything I would ever need, when I was changing career and setting up as a professional woodworker. Both those approaches were wrong. In an ideal world, by far the most cost- and time-

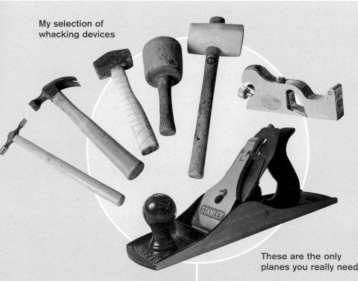

My selection of whacking devices

These are the only planes you really need

Using a scraper
plane to remove glue ooze

Scrapers are definitely an essential item if
you're going to use anything with irregular figuring

efficient method is to take a minimalist view and buy only good quality tools when the real need for them arises.

Let me take you on a tour of my workshop and describe some of my hand tools and why I have them.

BENCHES

In the early 1980s my brother, who is in the building business, alerted me to a local site where some useful scrap had been dumped, prior to burning, after a modernization programme at a local army site. I borrowed his pick-up, approached the contractor, and checked it out. I found the beech legs and rails for two benches, the softwood 3in (75mm) thick for the tops, some sheets of ¾in (10mm) ply and several four-drawer kitchen-unit pedestals.

I handed over some beer tokens to the contractor and brought it all home.After a bit of work I had constructed a very sturdy 2ft 9in x 8ft (840 x 2440mm) workbench and 3ft 6in x 8ft (1065 x 2440mm) assembly bench, both with drawers and shelves under.

The 3in (75mm)-thick softwood tops were covered with the ply, in turn covered with new hardboard, which is changed as necessary to keep a good clean, hard, smooth surface. Placed either side of my radial arm saw, they are still the centre of my hand-work activity.

HAMMERS AND MALLETS

Don't force it – get a bigger hammer! Apart from a pin and a claw hammer for general use, I have a carver's mallet, quickly turned from a piece of hornbeam from the log pile. This mallet was a temporary measure until I could afford a

'proper' one in lignum vitae, but it is still in frequent use and I have not felt the need to change it. There is also a 2½lb lump hammer and a rubber mallet.

In my previous existence I managed to 'bog in' a 4-ton anti-aircraft gun. After struggling for some time to pull it out with two four-ton trucks, I managed to bog them in as well, and had to summon help. This arrived in the form of a gnarled old transport sergeant with a 20-ton Scammel winch rescue truck. He pulled them all out to firm ground in a trice, like corks out of a bottle, muttering, 'Don't force it son – get a bigger hammer'.

This is a fundamental truth. In a restricted space a short swing from my 2½lb builder's club hammer can deliver all the force necessary, where any number of short blows from a smaller hammer can't.

But my favourite in the bashing department is the 'sand filled sock of the workshop' – my white rubber mallet. Some quite serious violence can be done with this when assembling or disassembling and it doesn't leave a mark!

WOODEN PLANES

Early on I had a collection of wooden planes, bought second-hand, which really looked the part – and that is about all they did. Moulding planes are made completely redundant by the router, and bench and smoothing planes are by far more accurate and easily adjustable in the metal versions. So I bought a no. 8 bench, a no. 5½ jack, and a no. 4 smoothing plane and spent hours fettling them up (thank you, David Charlesworth). In practice I found that the bench plane was replaced by the power planer with its longer tables, and the smoothing plane by the belt sander – I only really used the jack plane.

Sanding pads, blocks and abrasive file

My good set of chisels

A good sharp tap with some weight behind it often does the job better than a series of blows with a lighter hammer

Then I was lucky enough to be given a Lie-Nielsen no. 5 jack plane, which needed practically no fettling, stays sharp for ever and has hardly left my hands since. If only I had gone straight to that – the time and money I would have saved!

I also bought a flat and a curved spokeshave, a large and small rabbet, and a block plane. Of these, I find the flat spokeshave and small rabbet plane useful, and I use the others sometimes because they are there, but would not miss them if they weren't.

SCRAPERS

A scraper is always to hand for removing tears, finishing cross grain or interlocked grain, cleaning up, and removing glue ooze. I have several scrapers, some shaped for specific jobs, but only a small flexible type and a medium stiffer version are essential. My scraper plane helps to reduce 'burning thumbs' syndrome and is very useful on large pieces.

SANDING BLOCKS

Siafast Velcro-faced blocks, firm on one side and soft on the other, are quick and convenient for general sanding. I made wooden blocks to take sanding belts for situations that require more control than is possible on a belt sander. I have used a piece of sanding belt taped round a scraper to get in to awkward places and recently saw the abrasive file produced by Axminster Power Tool Centre, which

performs a similar function. It is very reasonably priced and has clips, which allow the strip of abrasive to be changed easily, so I bought one and find it extremely useful.

CHISELS

Chisels are often sold in sets and I am suspicious of this, as sets usually include something that you don't need. However my original purchase of a set of three (¾in, ½in and ¼in) plastic-handled chisels was a good buy.

I graduated to my selection of Ashley Isles chisels when I needed a better and more long-lasting edge. I bought the 1½in, 1in, ¾in, ½in, ⅜in, ¼in, ⅛in sizes one at a time as required, and I think they are worth every penny.

They are a delight to handle and use, hold an excellent edge, the backs are already polished and there is a free regrinding service, and for a small charge a refurbishing service. The chisels in the photo had just been reground and refurbished after 12 years of use. The original cheap set is still important – these are the chisels I mistreat! I keep them sharp, but not honed, in my 'often used' tool rack.

HOLDING DEVICES

Holding work still while glue sets or in order to operate on it with your hands, is probably one of the most important aspects of making. I have used everything from elaborate clamping arrangements to concrete blocks, sticky tape and hot glue. We will all come up with ingenious solutions to specific problems but there is a basic kit we should have.

Kevin's Top Tips

○ **Keep it clean!**

○ **Hardened glue on the clamps can make them difficult to adjust, and even mark the work.**

○ **Keep them clean – a rub over with candlewax on the moving parts helps them run free and adjust easily.**

○ **Do not use oil – it can mark the work and it collects dust.**

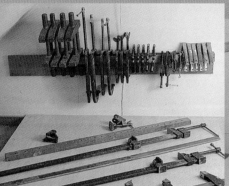

You can never have too many cramps and clamps – as long as they are the right ones

Sash cramps and band clamps in use

G-cramps and wooden cramps holding a curved door panel

SASH CLAMPS

These can be a tremendous expense but buying cheap sash clamps is a waste of money. Eight Record 3ft clamps cover the vast majority of my needs. For the occasional very large table or king-size bed I had 5 x 4ft (1525 x 1220mm) extension bars cut at a local steel works. I can bolt the clamps together, adjusting each end, or join them with the extension bars.

I also have four lighter 5ft Jet clamps that are very useful. Though the jaws cannot apply as much pressure as the sash clamps, they can reach further in to the work and can easily be reversed to form 'spreaders'. I had some lengths of suitable steel bar cut for these as the need arose. I also have two sets of clamp heads that I can use on wooden batons to make specific lengths of clamp as required.

'G' CLAMPS

I have a range of G-clamps, some picked up second-hand, and I use the 4in clamps most. The old-fashioned beech hand-screw clamps are kinder to the work and allow local pressure to be applied with the tips a fair way in, but will not give as much pressure as the steel clamps.

SPRING CLAMPS

Spring crocodile clips are quick and easy to use for light work, such as holding a moulding in position while the glue 'grabs'. They make a cheap and effective 'extra pair of hands'.

SPECIALIST CLAMPS

I use a pair of adjustable straps with hardwood blocks to clamp sets of corners and curved work; they also help clamp loads of timber onto the roof rack! Don't forget that concrete blocks make cheap weights to bear down on a stack of timber or a veneer. Hot glue can sometimes be used as a temporary fixing and cut through and cleaned off later, and of course sticky tape has solved many a clamping problem.

17 handtools you must have

My main vice (specific to woodworking, that is!) is in the centre of my work bench, has a 12in throat and a quick release, and can be fitted with hardwood cheeks lined with leather to protect the work. The tops of these cheeks have holes for bench dogs. A smaller vice with hardwood cheeks is fitted to the assembly bench. A metal 3in vice is fitted to the sharpening bench for metalwork.

BENCH HOLDING DEVICES

I do not have a tail vice, and have never missed it. The bench top has parallel lines of holes to take Veritas Wonder Dogs with a screw thread, so I can clamp work against a stop. The same holes also take a 'Holdfast' clamp. I also have two home-made bench hooks and a shooting board for mitres. Sometimes I open the drawers under the bench to help support long work held in the vice.

WOODEN BENCH DOG

A wooden bench dog is let through the bench and is normally left flush with the top. You can tap it through from underneath to give an adjustable stop, particularly for very thin work.

MEASURING IS A 'MUST'

Accurate measuring equipment is a 'must' and you do need a retractable spring steel tape. Make sure the hook on the end stays at right angles to the tape and use the same tape throughout the project. Or measure between two points on the tape, using say the 10in (255mm) line as the start point

Accurate tools for marking out and measuring are essential for fine work

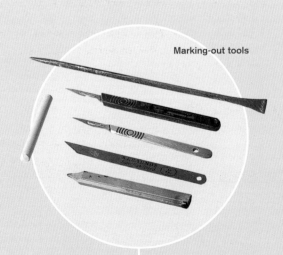

Marking-out tools

Dogs on your vice are a simple way
of providing a useful clamping method

Holdfast and adjustable bench dogs

and subtracting 10in (255mm) from the indicated
measurement. Allow for the thickness of the hook if taking
an internal measurement.I use a broken steel tape, the end
of which has been squeezed into a point, to measure
internal diagonals. It is easy to thread through clamps – the
point fits into corners, and I measure the difference in length
(rather than an actual measurement) of the diagonals. A
more sophisticated pointed end can be fixed to the tape but
I have not found it necessary.

RULES

A good 6in (150mm) or 12in (305mm) steel rule is ideal for
general accurate measurements. Metric and imperial scales
should be on the same rule with nice clear markings and
graduations chemically etched to last a lifetime. An anti-
glare, brushed chrome finish is preferable.

I also have a 1 metre metal rule, used as a straightedge
when marking out, and bent against pins or clamps to form
a curve to draw along.

I prefer the 6in (150mm) rule for general use and the
12in (305mm) rule on the combination square when
necessary.

STRAIGHTEDGE

A good steel straightedge is useful when setting up
machines or aligning tables, but not essential – it is perfectly
possible to make a straightedge from a piece of hardwood,
judged by eye.

SQUARES

A 3in (75mm) engineer's square is invaluable for setting out
and checking joints, fences, and blade alignment. Check it
by marking a vertical from a horizontal edge, with the base
of the square pointing to the right then turn the square over
so that the base is pointing to the left and see if the
square's edge runs parallel to the marked line. If it doesn't,
the square ain't square! I also have a 6in (150mm) square,
but it is not essential.

LARGE MARKING-OUT SQUARES

I use these to deal with sheets and large marking-out jobs.
Mine will locate on the edge and can be clamped and used
as a portable saw or router guide. I also use a carpenter's
square for internal measurements.

SLIDING COMBINATION SQUARE

This is a 12in (305mm) rule with a sliding try and mitre
square. It is a very cost-effective and useful tool that can be
used as an internal and external try and mitre square, a
depth or marking gauge, as well as a 12in (305mm) steel
rule, and straightedge. Mine even has a spirit level built in –
it was bought in the 1970s and is still in everyday use.

JAPANESE MITRE SQUARE

I bought this to set my table and radial arm saw blades
accurately to 45°, without taking the combination square to
pieces. Like the 3in (75mm) engineer's square, it is useful

for setting up and checking out. Its solid base allows it to be hooked against stock to measure mitres or stood up to check blades and fences. It's excellent value for money, but not essential.

CALLIPER

This instrument enables me to make accurate internal, external and depth measurements. The dial version is easier to read. Initially, I bought a plastic one but the jaws wore and it ceased to be accurate. I recommend the stronger stainless steel version.

ADJUSTABLE BEVEL

For a long time I just had an adjustable lockable bevel with the angles marked. It is not very accurate, but I used it to transfer the setting, rarely needing to know the actual angle. When angles are involved I draw the job full-size and take the angle off the drawing. However, recently I purchased a steel sliding protractor.

BAR GAUGE HEADS

Initially I thought these were a good idea used with sliding battens to take internal measurements, mainly of diagonals. But they proved almost impossible to use in clamping situations, so have been gathering dust ever since. My modified steel tape is far better.

LIGHTING

A portable light is useful in the workshop. Rechargeable lights are ideal and this Bosch version (right), which runs off a 24V drill battery is excellent. Keep a spare bulb though! Magnification is a great help when reading the finer graduations on measuring scales. Try a cheap pair of plastic x2 reading glasses or a magnifying lens.

MARKING

Where you use each piece of the available timber has a huge effect on the final item of furniture. I like to take my time to make the best use of what is available. Initial marking out is done with ordinary school chalk – easy to see and easy to rub out and change.

For more accurate work, I use a carpenter's thick pencil or just an ordinary HB one.

Where ultimate accuracy is required, particularly for marking out dovetails, I use a scalpel. A multitude of marking knives are available with fancy handles and permanent blades, which will require maintenance. I prefer scalpels – they are cheap and the replaceable blades are available in bulk.

MARKING GAUGES

I need at least two dedicated gauges, even though I could make do with a sliding combination square used with a pencil or a scalpel. Gauges with a blade, not a pin, are the best to use. Both need sharpening occasionally but I find the blade easier to sharpen, less likely to wander or follow the grain and less likely to tear when marking across the grain. Sharpen the blade like a chisel – a bevel on one side, flat on the other. Mark with the bevel to the waste side. I have a twin-pin mortice gauge but I cut my mortices by machine.

SAWS

I rarely cut anything by hand – most things are quicker and more accurate by machine saws. I made the mistake of buying expensive tenon, dovetail and gentleman's handsaws and – with the exception of the dovetail saw – hardly ever use them. Cheap modern hard-point saws seem ideal to me – just replace when blunt. It costs more to have the panel saw reset and sharpened than to buy several new hard-point versions.

Straightedges can be metal or wooden and large squares like the one in the middle can also be used as guides for routing and sawing. The easiest way to square things up diagonally is to use adjustable trammel bars

Measuring and setting up tools – note the pointed tape measure

Must haves

Claw hammer
Wooden mallet
No. 5 'jack' plane
Small shoulder plane
Medium scraper
¾, ½, ¼in paring chisels
Sash clamps 3' x 6
G-clamps 2 x 12in, 4 x 4in
10ft steel tape
6in steel rule
12in sliding combination square
I metre steel rule
Marking gauge (blade or cutting type) x 2
Scalpel and spare blades
Hard-point general purpose saw
Hard-point tenon saw or dovetail saw
Sanding blocks

Extra lighting and magnification can be helpful for marking out

Should haves

Small scraper
Spring clamps x 4
Modified steel tape for diagonals
3in engineering square
Metal vice
Protractor
Wooden adjustable bench dog
Holdfast
Second bench hook
Shooting board
Pin hammer
2½lb club hammer
White rubber mallet
Flat spokeshave
Scraper plane
Shaped scrapers
⅛in paring chisel
½in old chisel
6ft sash clamps (at least two)
Spring clamps (at least two)
Strap clamps (two)
Extension bars for sash clamps
x4 5ft Jet clamps & extension bars
x4 9in wooden screw clamps
Large marking-out square
Dial calliper
Adjustable bevel gauge
Portable light
x2 reading glasses
Hacksaw
Glue pot

Could haves

Assembly bench
Frame clamp
Japanese mitre square
Metal straightedge
Smoothing plane
Shaped scrapers
Steel adjustable protractor
Bar gauges
Anything specific to a job or your
    developed working practice as required

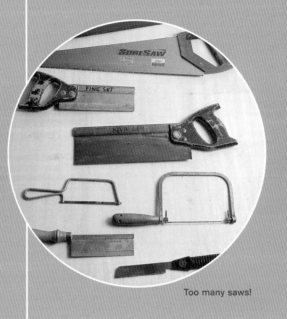

Too many saws!

I have a coping saw and a flush saw with a flexible blade and the teeth set only on one side to cut dowels off without marking the face – both of which I hardly ever use.

It would have been far more cost-effective to buy a general purpose and a dovetail hard-point saw, and a small hacksaw.

○ GLUE

The old days of the heated glue pot are long gone – modern glues are much stronger and more convenient. I often apply glue straight from a 'squeezy' bottle using a galvanized nail to plug the hole.

○ GENERAL

Keep all tools clean, sharp, properly adjusted, and in good repair. If they begin to rust then your workshop isn't suitable for them, you, or making furniture! Sort out the heat and moisture levels. Wooden or chipboard floors are better to work on and kinder to dropped tools – especially edge tools – chipped edges take a lot of repair. Choose tools specific to your needs and pocket, bearing in mind the fixed and portable power tools you have available. You get what you pay for – just make sure you are not paying for tools or features you do not need! I have made lists of hand tools I consider 'must haves', 'should haves' and 'could haves' for my way of making. These lists assume that you have a few portable and static machines, which I will cover later.

Static machinery 1

When I started making furniture in the early 1970s the only mechanical help I had was from the attachments one could get for the, then, ubiquitous Black & Decker drill. Soon I discovered the Myford combination machine in the base woodwork club and thought it was Christmas. A bandsaw, a 6in planer and a 6in circular saw. But it was too expensive to buy for myself and too big to ship around every time I was posted.

Once, when sharing a beer with an exchange USAF colonel at HQ strike command, lying about women and chatting in general, the conversation turned to DIY.

As nice as it is to have the best static machinery, Kevin shows you don't need to splash out to make great furniture

The colonel asked me which radial arm saw I had; apparently they were as common in the average American DIY workshop as the Black & Decker drill was in the UK. I had no idea what he was talking about so he showed me a Sears Roebuck catalogue, and this led to my first major purchase of woodworking machinery.

My attitude to machines is that they are for all the boring, hard, repetitive and non-creative work, leaving all the fun for me. Generally I find the 80/20 rule applies to buying machines; that means that 80% of the result is achieved with the first 20% of expenditure. It can be an expensive and pointless game chasing the optimum accuracy necessary for big batch work, when it simply isn't necessary. For a lot less money you can get most of the work done, and with a small amount of hand adjustment fine tune the result.

Another consideration is size. As floor space is always at a premium in my workshop the space occupied by any machine must be justified by its contribution to the end result. All of my larger machines are on wheels to give them more flexibility. For any purchase assess your needs and buy according to them.

Radial arm saw

Disc sanding on
the radial arm saw

Drum sanding on the RA
saw with dust extractor fitted

RADIAL ARM SAWS

When I started out there was nothing like the present range of power tools available, and they were relatively very expensive. Eventually I found in my price range a Craftsmen 10in radial arm saw, with a high-speed chuck power take off for use as an overhead router.

Very few attachments were available but my USAF chum got some imported from the States for me. Among them was a shaping head with a range of cutters. I still find it terrifying, and only ever use it as a last resort when wearing full body armour! There was also an adjustable dado head which is great, and still in use.

The Craftsmen was a good saw but it didn't hold its settings very well. So when I set up professionally I replaced it with the brand synonymous with RA saws – a DeWalt. The new saw held its settings, but was a bit fiddly to set up. Recently, after 16 years of faithful service, I replaced it with the new DW720K which arrived on a pallet, set up and bang on! Just as I like it – plug in, switch on and go!

CROSS CUTTING

RA saws are primarily designed to cross cut, which they do very accurately both horizontally and vertically. The blade can be adjusted to cut mitres, bevels or compound joints – a combination of both. The blade height can also be set to only cut part of the way through the work, enabling tenons and lap and kerf joints to be cut using multiple passes.

A negative-rake cross-cut blade helps prevent the blade 'climbing' the work, which can jam or stall the saw. A stop clamped to the fence makes very accurate repeat cuts simple. The hand holding the work against the fence should be at least 4in (102mm) away from the blade – do not move the work until the blade stops. Recent DW models have been fitted with a blade brake for safety and convenience.

RIPPING

The blade can be turned through 90° to become a large-capacity rip saw. This is useful for sheet material and large made-up panels, but impractical for any wany edged hardwood.

When ripping, it's essential to use the riving knife, anti-kickback fingers and pressure pad, as the blade can lift the work. Use a push stick to feed the end of the work through, turn the saw off and wait until the blade has stopped before moving the work.

DADO HEADS

A dado head is a blade on which the thickness can be adjusted to produce different widths of cut. It can be used to cut quick and accurate trenches, rebates, grooves and faster laps and tenons. I have the DeWalt dado accessory and use it regularly.

DRUM SANDING

The drum sander attachment can be used vertically or parallel to the table and gives a very stable platform from which to sand curves and straight lines accurately. The rip fence can be used to assist straight-line internal or external sanding and avoid a wavy edge or dwell marks. Relatively narrow pieces can be passed under the drum when parallel to the table, to edge, sand and 'thickness' at the same time.

Rounding over the back of blade on the
bandsaw with oilstone, blade turned by hand

Aligning bandsaw wheels with straight edge

DISC SANDING

The blade can be replaced with an 8in sanding disc faced
with self-adhesive sanding sheets. This can be set to any
angle required and be used to trim, adjust and shape ends.
Again it provides a stable platform for profile and face
sanding.

SAW BLADES

When rough cutting to length and ripping sheet material I
use a general-purpose 40-tooth TCT blade, when cross
cutting exactly, a negative-rake 80-tooth TCT blade and,
when ripping hardwood, a 25-tooth TCT rip blade.

USES

The first stage of reducing timber to a manageable size is
carried out on the RA saw, which is set up between my
assembly and my work benches, each over 8ft (2.4m) long
and all at the same height. This allows me to rough-cut
manageable lengths before processing them further.

Cross cutting, in one form or another, is the main use for
this machine, but the disc and drum sander facilities
enhance flexibility and save space. Although I use a
relatively cheap and small tablesaw for most standard
ripping jobs, a large-capacity rip or panel saw is very useful
for specific situations. If I could have only one static
machine this would be it, and I would have to buy my timber
planed all round.

A home-made
wheel conversion

PLANER THICKNESSERS

For me, the second most important machine is the planer
thicknesser. Basic economics, conservation and my love of
native hardwoods – and showing them off to their best
advantage – necessitate maximum control of cutting out.
The waste, which is trimmed to make straight-edged
boards, might not have been waste to me and I will have
paid for it to be cut off and thrown away. At least my
workshop waste goes on to the wood burner!

To achieve the end result I want, I need to be able to
face, edge and thickness timber in the workshop. I see little
point in having a planer without the thicknessing facility, but
they are available as a jointer (surface planer) and a
separate thicknessing machine.

DONKEY WORK

The amount of boring, hard work the planer thicknesser
saves is phenomenal. Imagine facing and thicknessing by
hand enough timber for a small coffee table, let alone a
decent-sized bedroom suite! Flat surfaces, even thicknesses
and straight edges are essential to give a base from which
to take accurate measurements.

SIZE MATTERS

Plenty of machines are available in a range of sizes and all
will be a compromise in one way or another. Once the blade
size reaches 12in the rest of the machine tends to be built
to a professional standard with cast-iron tables of a decent
length. The longer the tables the easier it is to get a straight
edge on a long board. It is all a matter of 'you get what you
pay for' but I would rather have a smaller, lighter machine
than none at all.

Kevin's Top Tips

○ Ensure you always use sharp blades.

○ Check the machine settings before use.

○ Make a test cut and confirm settings.

○ Do not overload – a series of shallow passes are kinder, safer and more accurate than forcing through one deep cut.

○ Maintain machines regularly; adjust drive belts, tighten nuts and bolts, and wax tables and screw threads.

Kevin's radial arm saw in rip mode, with push stick. Note that the anti-kickback fingers, pressure pad, and riving knife are in position

Touching up planer blades in situ

RA saw, sanding disc and drum, dado heads, fence stop and home-made dust hood

SETTING UP

The most crucial factor on this machine is the blades. They must be sharp, clean and set accurately in relation to the outfeed table.

To set the blade height, hold a steel rule on the outfeed table and rotate the cutter block past it, adjusting the blade height until, as the blade passes the rule, it moves it forward by ³⁄₆₄in (1mm). Set this height at each end of each blade and tighten the holding bolts from the centre outwards to avoid distortion, checking the blade height after the bolts have been tightened.

If the blade is set too low the work may foul the outfeed table edge, resulting in a step on the beginning of a surfacing pass; too high will give a similar step on the other end.

SHARPENING

I have two sets of blades, one on the machine and one sharp set ready to replace them. Each set must be ground at the same time so that they remain the same size and weight to avoid vibration. After they have been ground I polish the backs on a coarse water stone to hone the edge and remove any burr.

The blades can be touched up on the machine with a stone. Stick tape on the outfeed table to protect it and wedge the blades in position with a wooden block. I regard this as an emergency measure, or fine tuning for a particularly difficult piece. If the blades are blunt it is time to change them for sharp ones!

THICKNESSING

Provided you have correctly set the blades, accurately thicknessed work should be the same depth on each side. If not then there is a problem in the alignment of the blades and the thicknessing tables.

USE

A number of shallow passes rather than one deep one give a better finish and avoid overloading the machine. Keep the tables clean and wipe off any resin build-up with white spirit. Reduce table friction by rubbing it lightly with candle wax. Use roller stands when dealing with long pieces on the surfacer or the thicknesser.

Static
machinery 2

Prolong your career and keep all your digits by taking care with static machinery in the workshop and using some form of dust extraction.

Bandsaws are probably the most basic machine, but are very versatile for their size, as in deep sawing here

DUST EXTRACTION

The planer-thicknesser is the machine which really underlines the need for some sort of dust and chip collector. So much waste is produced that neither you nor the machine can work properly or safely without one. There are many dust extractors on the market, and it is important to understand which is suitable for your needs.

They fall into three types:

① HIGH-VOLUME LOW-PRESSURE

This type moves a large volume of air at low pressure, has a coarse filter, and is most suitable for collecting chips and coarse dust. The hose diameter is approximately 3in (75mm), and any reduction in that or increase in length markedly reduces efficiency.

They are often used for planer-thicknessers and ripsaws, which produce large quantities of chips rather than fine dust. Although they collect most of the waste, unfortunately the fine dust they let through is the most harmful. Breathing masks are, therefore, still essential. They have a large waste capacity, but do take up workshop space.

Aligning bandsaw wheels with straightedge

② LOW-VOLUME HIGH-PRESSURE

These are more like large domestic vacuum cleaners, shifting a smaller volume of air at a much higher pressure. The maximum hose diameter is 2in (50mm), and the filter system goes right down to very fine dust.

However, they have a relatively small waste capacity making them more suitable for belt sanders and routers. Anything producing bulk shavings will either clog the narrower hoses or fill them up very quickly. Usually on wheels, they are very convenient to move around and take up little space.

③ HIGH-VOLUME HIGH-PRESSURE

These are bigger versions of the last type with very powerful motors. Suitable for remote static siting, they can also be connected to a ducted system. This is where the machines are all permanently plumbed in and controlled by opening and closing blast gates, applying the dust collection to the relevant machine.

Able to handle large quantities of mixed chips and fine dust, the hoses can be stepped right down to 1in (25mm) for a belt sander or up to 4in (100mm) for the ripsaw and planer. However, when exclusively producing large volumes of fine dust, like during belt sanding, the fine filter end clogs and the machine loses efficiency.

Emptying, changing and cleaning the filter is a bit of an inconvenience, so I have recently bought a small low-volume high-pressure extractor to use on fine dust producers. It is cheaper and quieter to run, portable, and much easier to empty and clean. It also has the added advantage of an electrical socket for the power tool, which automatically switches the extractor on and off with the power tool switching.

⚪ BANDSAW

My first bandsaw was really only DIY standard and I quickly found it would not do what I wanted. On its stand it took up the same floor space as a machine of much greater capacity, and being lighter it was not so stable.

Apart from the standard bandsaw cut, I needed to deep-saw burr elm for book-matched panels, cedar of Lebanon for drawer casings, and saw-cut veneers. Also, any timber of 3in (75mm) or more in thickness was really beyond the capacity of my other saws, so I wanted a big bandsaw with plenty of power.

I chose the Electra Beckum 450 with a 17in (430mm) throat and 12in (305mm) depth of cut, backed by a powerful motor. This has served me well over the last 16 years, though the aluminium table and fences are a bit naff. I notice a new version of this machine – the BAS 600 – has a cast-iron table and micro-adjustable fence, which would be even better.

When setting up, check the wheel alignment by placing a straightedge across the rims – it should touch the top and bottom of each wheel at the same time. The blade should run on the centre of the wheel tyres. Blade tension, guides and thrust bearings should all be set accurately to the manufacturer's instructions.

⚪ BLADES

As usual, the most important factor is a sharp, suitable blade. Trying to cut too tight a radius with a wide blade, a straight line with a narrow one, or burning your way through the wood with a blunt blade is slow and inaccurate.

Ripping is most
accurate on a table saw

Drilling large holes accurately, like this
35mm hole, can really only be done on a pillar drill

The wider the blade, the straighter the cut. Conversely, the narrower the blade, the tighter the curve it can cut. The greater the number of teeth to the inch, the slower and finer the cut, and the hotter the blade gets.

I find a ½in, 4 or 6 TPI blade most suitable for general work and deep-sawing. I have narrower blades for tighter curves and even a very fine-toothed blade for cutting sheet metal. I have always used blades with hardened teeth, which are disposable and cannot be sharpened. The backs of the blades are rounded over with an oilstone to allow slightly tighter turns and protect the thrust bearings.

CIRCULAR TABLE SAW

As the RA saw is to crosscutting, so the table saw is to ripping. I don't do anything fancy on mine, just use it for what it is really good at – ripping straight lines. My present DeWalt 744 is very flexible, having a rack-and-pinion telescopic fence system and extension tables. These give over 2ft (600mm) rip capacity when required, but all slot back into the machine out of the way when not in use. On its stand, it is stable but still easily moved. I use a 24-tooth TCT blade – incidentally, remember that even TCT blades get blunt and require sharpening occasionally!

When using the circular saw, remember not to stand in the line of fire behind the work – use roller stands at both ends for long pieces, and push sticks to keep fingers clear of the teeth.

LATHE

My Elu lathe is nearly 20 years old, and was only ever of serious hobbyist standard. Nevertheless, it has served me well over the years – even though its prime function has only been drawer pulls, dowel pegs and bun feet.

This is a rarely used tool, but still necessary for convenience. I have a very basic range of tools and use all the help I can get, including: profile finders, rods to mark cut positions and, most of all, sizing tools to achieve constant diameters.

Like any infrequently used skill, there is always an initial learning curve so I try to do all the turning for any project in one batch, with extra 'insurance' pieces.

SHARPENING TURNING TOOLS

A long time ago, I turned a few natural-edged burr elm bowls to serve as impulse buys when displaying my work in a local show. Admiring them, a recently redundant miner told me that he was trying to develop his turning hobby into a business, but was finding it difficult to do fast, accurate work, and would I take him on as a student!

Aware of my limited turning skills, I kept an absolutely straight face and, calling upon every ounce of my military training, I made vague excuses, but he was very insistent. Clutching wildly at straws, I asked how often he sharpened his turning tools: 'Every week without fail', he said.

Now on safe ground, I replied with great relief: 'Well I sharpen mine about every five minutes,' and with no loss of face, sent away a satisfied customer. Sharp tools are always the secret.

Kevin's Top Tips

- Set guards and kickback devices correctly.
- Use dust extraction.
- Keep the area around machines clear.
- Ensure work is properly supported.
- Clear shavings and dust away from machine areas.
- Use pushsticks.
- Keep fingers at least 4in (100mm) away from the whirling knives and blades!

Lathe with sizing tools, profile copier, marking rods, and dust extraction hose

Slot morticing on a planer can limit space and cause a few bruises!

A bench morticer takes up less space

BENCH DRILL

Bench drills can give truly vertical holes, accurate angle drilling, repeats, safe large-diameter drilling, and – with suitable attachments – even morticing. All this, and they are still amazingly cheap.

For a very reasonable price you can get a substantial multi-speed model. Attachments such as machine vices and table clamps are also inexpensive and readily available to purchase.

These bench drills may not have the absolute accuracy required for aircraft engineering, but they are much better than freehand – I wouldn't be without mine.

BENCH MORTICER

Over the last few years I have found myself using my slot morticer attachment on the planer-thicknesser less and less, and smacking myself on the handles more and more. The router and biscuit jointer were taking over.

When I changed my planer-thicknesser, I did not get the slot-morticing attachment and saved some floor space – and bruises. I considered a morticing attachment for my pillar drill, but found a bench morticer more substantial, more accurate, and easier to use.

It has the added advantage of being quite compact, and can be stored under the bench until required. It is slower than the slot morticer, but will only be used occasionally.

CONCLUSION

Static machines take the hard labour out of the workshop, and make our work economically viable. There is no shame in using machines – in fact, many tasks are actually better and more accurately done by machine. They also release us to provide the creative and artistic input, maximizing our contribution to the added value.

I try not to be too obsessive about all aspects of accuracy – wood is inherently inaccurate in that it moves as its moisture content changes anyway. Better to concentrate on the really important areas rather than pedantically chasing horizons. For instance, I often cut tenons slightly oversize on the machine and trim with a shoulder plane to a perfect fit for each mortice.

Remember that about 750 watts of electrical power equals one horse power. Most static machines are at least two horse power, and imagining yourself to be at the back end of a couple of frisky horses will focus the mind on the potential danger quite well! If you do something unusual on a machine – especially if it involves removing a guard – think it through very carefully, and always keep all your fingers at least 4in (100mm) away from the blade!

Portable power tools 1

There is a huge range of portable power tools and accessories now available to us all. They are cheaper, better, and more versatile than ever, with accessories which often extend their use even further. We can expand our creative horizons and remove much of the time-consuming drudgery from some of the more repetitious tasks. There is nothing wrong with using these labour-saving devices; if the Georgian or Shaker makers had access to them they would undoubtedly have made even more beautiful furniture; indeed the Shakers invented the first circular saws.

There can be a high 'toys for the boys' factor here, and even though I try not to be a tools groupie there is always the danger of buying for the wrong reasons.

In the next two sections I will take a hard look at the portable power tools and their accessories that I find really useful in my workshop, and the rationale for buying them. I will also admit some of my mistaken buys and hopefully this will help readers understand which bits of kit – and what level of financial outlay – they really need to improve their creative workflow and the potential scope of their projects.

The router has transformed furniture making practices and become an essential tool in the workshop

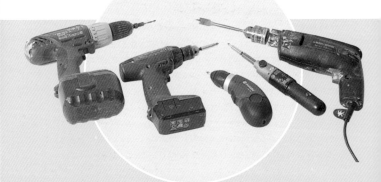

Kevin's collection of drills and drivers

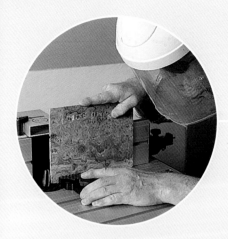

Raising a fielded panel with a vertical
cutter wearing the Clearflow Turbovisor

Belt sanding with DeWalt and sanding
frame saving hours of handwork

Orbital sanding with
a Bosch palm sander

PRINCIPLES OF PURCHASES

When buying power tools I apply the following
basic principles:

⊙ SUITABILITY

This may seem obvious but the tool must do what it is
supposed to do simply, safely and accurately. Some of the
entry-level kit does not, and can be a waste of time and
money. One is better off doing the job the long way round
by hand, or spending the extra money to achieve a
proper result.

⊙ VALUE FOR MONEY

Make sure you are not paying for features or capacity you
will never use. For example a 4in belt sander, designed to
sand floors all day, is overkill for the average one-man
furniture workshop. It will cost twice as much and can be
excessively heavy and difficult to use on edges and in
restricted areas.

⊙ TECHNICAL ASSISTANCE, ACCESSORIES AND SPARES

Make sure that motor brushes, drive belts, switches and
other known routine spares are readily available and
reasonably priced. Ensure that technical help is easy to
access and that any accessories you may need are
available. I was once looking at a fairly expensive belt
sander; it did not have a sanding frame, which I consider
essential, but the salesman assured me they were 'probably
working on one'! Check the prices of accessories. Very
often, attractive discounts on the main item are not repeated
on spares and accessories. Sometimes a 'bundle' or
'package' offer will be a bargain, or if you are sure you
know what you want, you can drive a bargain for buying it
all together.

⊙ INSURANCE

As you read on you will see that I sometimes have
duplicates of similar tools. There are several reasons for
this; sometimes the two apparently similar items have
different features that I find useful, and sometimes different
settings need to be preserved on each item for a particular
job. As tools only break when in use and, irritatingly, when
they are absolutely essential to a critical deadline, a second
'just in case' piece of kit can be a life-saver. I know it's a bit
of a luxury but it's how I earn my living!

THE TOOLS

⊙ ELECTRIC DRILLS

These were the original portable power tools of the 1970s.
A huge range of attachments was available, all using the
drill motor for power, including drum, disc and orbital
sanders, circular and jigsaws, routers, hole saws and even
a lathe – all with varying degrees of efficacy, quality,
convenience and safety. Strangely, in the light of modern
usage, screwdriver attachments were not so popular, at
least until speed control and the Phillips and Posidrive
heads came along. Nowadays the cordless drill/driver is a
very useful tool specifically for drilling holes and driving
screws. Thankfully nowadays far more versatile and
effective dedicated tools have replaced the range of, frankly,
generally substandard attachments.

⊙ DRILLS

My mains drill hasn't been out of its drawer in years now.
My big Bosch 24V cordless is convenient and has plenty of
power and duration for the big jobs, but it is heavy and can
be difficult to control on lighter tasks. Its little brother, the

Cordless drills and drivers are
a boon in tight fitting situations

Trend's mortice and tenon jig proved
its worth on a multiple run of chair tenons

Bosch 7V, is light, small, easily controlled, and has ample power and duration for the majority of cabinetmaking tasks. I use it as both a drill and a screwdriver.

DRIVERS

I have two dedicated drivers, the ergonomically shaped Metabo 4.8V Powergrip, and my original tiny 2.4V Black & Decker power screwdriver, which is really on its last legs. I find the Powergrip easy to use and with ample power and control for most of my work – and a godsend when fitting piano hinges!

ROUTERS

My routing system is based on the Trend range. The company is based in the UK and it has a great range of accessories, a good technical department, sensible prices, quick delivery and helpful staff. There may be others as good but my router experiences have been with Trend for some years, so I speak as I find.

GENERAL-PURPOSE ROUTER

My smaller router is the versatile T5, which though similar to the ubiquitous old Elu MOF 96 – unfortunately no longer available in the UK – that so many of us started with in days of yore, is much updated and improved. This is the smallest router I consider a worthwhile buy. Below this level I have found irritating little faults like play on plunge bars, poor adjustment and a general lack of power. Features I find particularly useful are the side-fence micro-adjustment, fine-height adjustment, soft start, and its full range of

accessories. For me its main uses are for light and hand-held work, though it will also fit the router table and has up to an 8mm collet, meaning it can be used for a much wider variety of tasks. It is light, easy to use and control, with good visibility of the cutting area, and provides dust extraction.

HEAVY-DUTY ROUTER

I purchased the 1800W T9 as a replacement for my first router, an old Elu MOF 98 that lasted me for 15 years. The improvement in routers that had taken place was very apparent on the T9, which also has soft start, micro adjustments, and is ideal for heavier work and long runs. I use it mainly on the router table for work such as fielding panels, deeper passes for slotting, and larger mouldings. Off the table it is used for cutting mortices. A full range of collet sizes up to ½in, including all the metric and imperial sizes is available – useful for those of us who started our cutter collections in old money!

ROUTER ACCESSORIES

CUTTERS

In the main I use tungsten-carbide-tipped cutters – they stay sharper longer – and go for the largest-diameter shanks which are stronger and grip more firmly in the collet. I hone the edges by polishing the back (non-bevel side) with a small diamond whetstone – a couple of strokes before each use prolongs the time needed between professional sharpening.

Do not be shy about using portable power tools – if the Georgian makers had them, they would have made even more beautiful furniture.

Router with biscuits and wafers of different sizes

Pulsafe Clearflow Turbovisor and power pack, a necessary item for any machining

RANGE OF CUTTERS

This is a matter of personal preference, but I would advise against buying sets, and simply build up a collection on an 'as required' basis. I use very few moulding cutters, but would not be without my rounding-over, vertical panel and straight cutters.

ROUTER TABLE

This is an invaluable aid in increasing the scope, accuracy and safety of router operations. They can be made quite simply but, as it saved me the cost of a spindle moulder and given that I'd rather make furniture anyway, I bought mine!

JIGS

Router use can be greatly extended by the use of jigs – indeed some people spend more time making jigs for their routers than doing anything else! Many are available, from simple stops on the fence or table for repeated runs, to complex, expensive, commercial multi-joint jigs. One should balance the time taken to make or the expense of buying the jig against the time/money saved by using it.

JOINT JIGS

I love making the joints in my furniture by hand but find the router very useful for removing the bulk of the waste, leaving me to do the final chiselling for an accurate fit.

The signature of hand-made furniture is the hand-made joint, and the essence of those joints is the final hand tailoring to fit, rather than the labour of hacking out the bulk

of the waste. There are many dovetail jigs available – some produce dovetails almost good enough to have been done by hand, but they cost, take up space, and by the time I have set them up I could probably have done the job anyway.

I do have the Trend mortice-and-tenon jig, which I bought specifically for a run of compound joints for a set of eight chairs. It paid for itself on that one run and was, in my opinion, good value for money. I was very careful setting it up, doing several test pieces, which took some time, then used undersized cutters and hand trimmed the joints to an exact fit. An oversize tenon is simple to adjust but an undersize one is not!

GUIDES

To guide the routers for housing joints and trenching in general, outside the range of the fitted fence, I have a number of methods: a home-made clamp guide, a shiny aluminium larger version, and a combined T square and guide which can be G-cramped in place.

CONCLUSION

My drills, drivers and routing equipment are essential elements in my making where balancing the time and cost of achieving the client's requirements is so important. In the next section I will cover the rest of my range of power tools, starting with my very favourite time and effort savers – the sanders.

Portable power tools 2

In the last section I began covering the range of power tools I have in my workshop with my drills, screwdrivers, and routing set-up. Now I will continue with the apples of my one remaining eye – the sanders. For sheer value of time saved you can't beat power sanding.

Keeping you away from slavery, beltsanding edges with the Makita

BELT SANDERS

I have two 3in belt sanders – the DeWalt DW431 and the Makita 9903. They take the same size belts, have adjustable speeds, similar power and good dust extraction. Both are excellent at their primary task of sanding large and small areas flat. The Makita comes with a side fence which is very useful on edges, and the DeWalt a cross fence which I seldom use.

ACCESSORIES

I have a sanding frame for each and prefer the DeWalt – it is better made and easier to adjust. The DeWalt requires a stand to use it inverted and I find it a bit rich that the plastic dust extraction spout is an extra. The Makita does not require an inversion stand, though one is available. It has a flat top, can stand inverted on the bench, and will connect directly to a dust extractor. The only other accessories I have are the belts, of which I have a range of cloth-backed, aluminium oxide-coated, from 40 grit to 150 grit.

ORBITAL SANDERS

My mainstay in this department is the powerful Bosch 400AE random orbital disc sander. It has variable speed so it can be used over a wide range of sanding operations from serious stock removal on full speed with 60-grit discs, to denibbing with a 240 disc at minimum speed to avoid over-heating, and melting the varnish.

Kevin's collection of belt sanders and accessories

Orbital sanding with
Bosch micro filter

Biscuit jointing
with the Trend T20

Using the Pulsafe
Clearflow Turbovisor

To complement the random orbital, I have a Bosch palm sander which is better on square and rounded-over edges and, being smaller, is easier to use in some less-accessible areas.

Because it tends to remove much less stock, dust extraction is not so important so I can use the Bosch Microfilter system and not need a vacuum hose. The smaller oscillations also enable it to be used right up to a vertical edge like the raised edge of a fielded panel.

I also have an Elu ⅓ sheet orbital sander which I bought before random orbitals were invented and which is still going strong, but not much used these days – random orbitals don't leave that mass of comma-shaped marks in the surface!

BISCUIT JOINTER

It took ages for me to cotton on to the advantages of the biscuit jointer, but I wouldn't be without one now. I also make good use of Tanseli wafers, sometimes using the biscuit jointer to cut the long slot and sometimes a 4mm cutter on the router.

The biscuit jointer is one of those machines that is sublimely simple and does what it is supposed to do – cut a slot in the right place consistently and accurately – very well indeed with no accessories or complications. Some say it is only suited to MDF and other sheet materials and has no place in solid wood construction but I disagree and find myriad uses for it.

I have one mid-range Trend T20 jointer which does the job for me. Back up in an emergency would be the router, but all the convenience would have gone and the jointer would have to be back in operation in quick time.

VACUUM CLEANER

Most of the preceding power tools produce a lot of dust, so a small powerful vacuum cleaner/dust extractor is essential – the more powerful the better, particularly for routers where it is difficult to get dust extraction nozzles close to the source, and which can produce huge amounts of dust and chippings.

I have the Trend T30 vacuum dust extractor which comes with all the fittings for the routers and cleaning the workshop floor and fits all my sanders as well. It is more effective and convenient than stepping down the 4in hose of my plumbed-in extraction system for dust extraction on sanders or routers.

PULSAFE CLEARFLOW TURBOVISOR

There are some occasions when, despite the best efforts of all the dust extraction systems in the workshop, there is still a lot of dust about. It is difficult to efficiently extract dust when sanding on the lathe and on some routing operations. This is where my over-pressure helmet with whole face safety visor comes into play. It has a rechargeable power pack that clips onto the belt and runs for some hours. The dust-free filtered air is directed down the front of the visor for demisting and delivered to the mouth and nose. The visor gives excellent eye and face protection and the whole thing is relatively comfortable to wear. Mine is in frequent use when I am working on the lathe or routing and really came into its own recently when I was hand sanding a lot of zebrano, the dust from which is particularly unpleasant. It was also very useful when insulating a loft with fibreglass some time ago!

Dust extractor and fittings

RECHARGEABLE LAMP

I bought my Bosch 24V drill as part of a set that included a rechargeable lamp and a sabre saw all running off the same size battery. The lamp is an absolute wonder. It has an adjustable head that can be directed onto all those difficult-to-light spots, such as under tables, that exist even in the most well lit of workshops. Running off a 24V drill battery it is very bright and lasts forever on one charge. Beware though – the bulbs can be a bit fragile and tend to blow if the lamp is dropped. They are expensive, and not easy to buy over the counter so I keep a couple in stock.

DEHUMIDIFIER

Damp workshops and furniture making are not happy co-habitees. I have an Ebac dehumidifier in the workshop and another in the wood store to keep the relative humidity levels down. Both run at night on the cheap electricity when all the doors and windows are closed and they are at their most effective, as the air change rate and movement is at its lowest.

CHAIN SAW

In a previous life my squadron was issued with 12 chain saws with 26in bars to clear sites for missile launchers. No instructions or safety kit came with them; somebody at staff level had obviously thought it a 'good idea'. Just like buying one over the counter in civilian life.

I contacted the local Forestry Commission and they kindly trained one of my sergeants as an instructor to train the operators. In true military tradition he brought back a horror film of chain saw injuries which caused us to treat the saws with the same respect as a machine gun. He began his training sessions with the droll warning: 'Chain saws don't nip – they take the whole piece.'

I do have one, mainly for logging for the wood burner, but I can see little justification for one in the average workshop. If you feel it essential, then get the smallest one you can to suit your needs, get trained, and wear full protective gear when using it. Some manufacturers or retailers provide training on request.

JIGSAW

I bought a jigsaw in a fit of enthusiasm when I turned pro, but have found very little use for it over the years. It seems inherently inaccurate to me and the job is far better done a different way, for instance on the bandsaw, with a router, or by hand.

SORTING THE WHEAT FROM THE CHAFF

In the table below I have listed my power tools by relative importance to my operation. I have identified them by make and model so that the specifications are clear. Other makes or models may be preferred, but these are the power tools that I find serve my purposes.

ESSENTIAL	DESIRABLE	SURPLUS
Trend T9 router	Trend T5 router	Bosch GSA24 VE cordless sabre saw
Trend PRT router table	Trend MT/JIG	Black and Decker 9018 2.4V screwdriver
Trend router guide clamp	Trend T-square and guide	Black and Decker DN36 jigsaw
DW 431 belt sander	Makita 9903 belt sander	Skil chainsaw
DW DE 4070 sander frame	Makita sanding shoe (frame)	Elu MVS 156 orbital sander
DW DE4051 sander inversion stand	Bosch GSS 16A palm sander	
Bosch PEX 400AE random orbital sander	Bosch Micro-filter system	
Bosch GLI 24V rechargeable lamp	Ebac Humidex small dehumidifier for wood store	
Ebac Home Dry 660 dehumidifier for workshop	Bosch GSR24E2 drill/driver	
Black and Decker 162 mains drill	Clearflow Turbovisor	
Bosch PSR 7.2 VE 7V drill/driver		
Metabo Powergrip screwdriver		
Trend T30 vacuum cleaner dust extractor		

Dehumidifier in wood store

SABRE SAW

The cordless sabre saw which came as part of the Bosch drill and lamp set seemed a great idea in theory for cutting in the wood store, or rough-cutting sheets or planks to manageable sizes to get up the stairs to the workshop. But in reality I very seldom need it, and those jobs can be done better by hand anyway.

It is a site tool that would be very useful to joiners, or kitchen or window fitters. Its main use for me is pruning our trees!

CONCLUSION

Power tools are wonderful time and effort savers, often making a piece of furniture economically viable. Hand planing, scraping and sanding a large piece in a wild-grained hardwood could easily double its price, and the commission lost. The skill required in using power tools is no less than using hand tools, just different. We should not make the mistake of some of the early purist Arts and Crafts furniture makers who rejected machinery and power tools, insisting all making should be done with hand tools. They priced themselves out of the market.

Projects

Play

on

Project 1 Project

The cabinet featured here was a commission for a client and was to match some brown oak and sycamore bookcases that I had already made for him. A walnut and burr elm desk which was another commission, is also in the same sitting room – fortunately, the bookcases are on either side of the substantial chimney breast and do not intrude into the floor space, and the room is well-proportioned with a bay window and high ceiling, and big enough to take these four pieces!

DESIGN

The design of the cabinet started from the inside – the most important aspect, of course, was that it would take all the client's hi-fi units, tape cassettes, CDs and vinyl LPs. He particularly wanted glazed doors so as to reduce dusting, and he wanted to be able to see all the hi-fi units through the glass, without the fronts being obscured by the frames.

Venting for heat dissipation, and access at the back for plugs and leads, would also be required. The CDs and tape cassettes were to be stored in drawers, and the LPs on the partitioned shelf with a glazed drop front.

The client decided to relate this unit more to the bookcases than the desk, and base it on the same simple straightforward design, reflecting the traditional, solid stone construction of the 18th-century house.

We measured the drawer space required for his CDs, LPs and tape cassettes, and I borrowed his catalogue for the hi-fi components for their dimensions.

It took some time to draw up the final design on the computer – the components were arranged into two equal height stacks with a plinth to raise them above the bottom rail for the door frame. The vents were placed carefully to allow them to double as access holes for the leads and plugs, and the back was set in 2⅜in (60mm) leaving a reveal to house and hide them.

Contrasting timbers are designed to break up an otherwise heavy piece

Back showing venting
and reveal to hide wiring

Doors open showing
interior layout

TIMBER

The bookcases had been delivered before this piece was conceived and the client was pleased with the timber combination. So this cabinet would also be constructed with a brown oak (*Quercus spp*) carcass, sycamore (Acer pseudoplatanus) back and component stack plinths, with ripple sycamore drawer fronts and frames to the glazed doors and drop flap.

Brown oak is normal English oak which has been attacked by the Beef Steak fungus (*Fistulian hepatica*). This fungus enters through an open wound or damaged area and, though it feeds off the tree, it does little damage, taking sustenance from the sap and excreting waste chemicals into the wood which cause the attractive change of colour to a rich, dark, golden brown.

Ripple sycamore is the same creamy-white colour as ordinary sycamore, with a similar uniform, straight-grain, a fine close even texture, and a natural lustre. It also has an even mass of ripple grain running at right angles to the grain of the wood. The cause is not know and it is not possible to tell if it is present until the tree is cut. You will sometimes see holes in the side of sycamore trees where the buyer of the standing timber has taken a plug of wood out to check!

The ripple is much more valuable and is prized by musical instrument makers – in fact it is sometimes called 'fiddle-back sycamore'.

When I bought the brown oak and ripple sycamore for the bookcases, the quality had been so good that I had bought extra and had sufficient of all three to do this cabinet. The quarter-sawn brown oak was very nice – of even colour and with few faults – the sycamore and ripple sycamore came in good clean, wide boards, also with few faults.

I had checked when I bought the sycamore that it had been end-reared and that the stick marks did not penetrate too far. Having used some of this batch for the bookcases, I knew that there would be no problems with thias. The sycamore-faced MDF for the backs was ordered locally.

TIMBER PREPARATION

The timber is marked out and cut slightly over-size, stacked with stickers between the boards, and left in the timber store, equipped with a dehumidifier, for a couple of weeks or so to settle.

Final conditioning takes place in the workshop, where the temperature and relative humidity should be kept as close as possible to the final end-use conditions. This helps avoid movement problems later.

CARCASS CONSTRUCTION

All the components are faced and thicknessed, then those pieces requiring it are made up to width from narrower boards, edge jointed with biscuit reinforcing.

The frames to go between the drawers are also made up using biscuits glued at the front but not at the back, leaving an expansion gap to allow for future movement.

The shelves and drawer frames are fitted into stopped housing in the sides and partition, cut with a router ⅞in (22mm) wide by ⅜in (9mm) deep. The same applies to the sides and partition, fitting to the top and base.

PARTITIONS

The partitions in the LP compartment are made up from two pieces of ¼in (5mm) sycamore-faced MDF, glued back-to-back and lipped with solid sycamore. The lip is 3in (75mm) deep to allow for the biscuits reinforcing the join, and the curved front. They are cut to size and shape, shouldered, and fitted into the stopped housings in the shelves above and below. As they are to be finished with an acrylic varnish to preserve the creamy colour, and the brown oak around them to be oiled, they are finished and given three coats of varnish before assembly.

The ¼in (5mm) slots for the back are cut in the sides and top, set in 2⅜in (60mm) to leave the reveal to hide the wires and plugs.

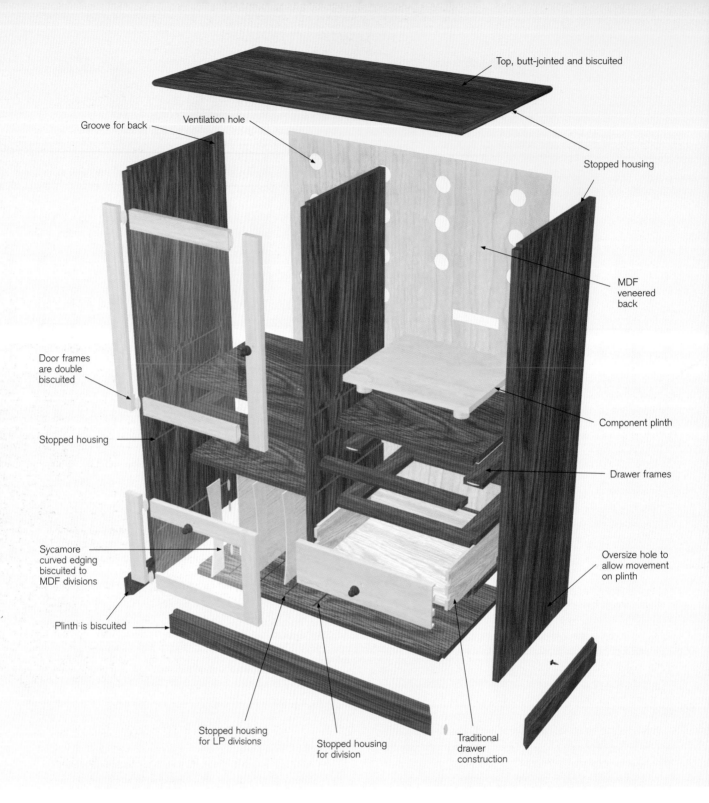

Top, butt-jointed and biscuited

Groove for back

Ventilation hole

Stopped housing

MDF veneered back

Door frames are double biscuited

Stopped housing

Component plinth

Drawer frames

Sycamore curved edging biscuited to MDF divisions

Oversize hole to allow movement on plinth

Plinth is biscuited

Stopped housing for LP divisions

Stopped housing for division

Traditional drawer construction

⊚ ASSEMBLY

Do a trial dry assembly to check that the shelves, drawer frames, LP partitions and base fit properly into their respective stopped housings.

Prepare the clamps and equipment and, above all, allow plenty of time. There is a lot to put together at once and it is all quite big and heavy – not a Friday afternoon job! Apply Titebond to the stopped housings, and clamp. Check the diagonals at the back and front to check for square. The partition is chocked as, unlike the sides, it does not touch the floor. Check the horizontal line of the shelves and drawer frames to make sure that there is no sag.

Preparation is important – it often takes longer than you think, but is worth doing carefully.

Finally, leave it all to set.

Top cramped-up using cauls

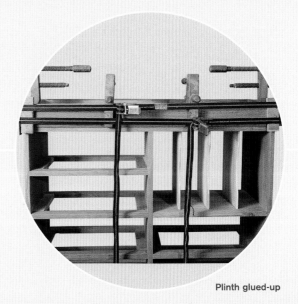
Plinth glued-up

Plinth

Now that the carcass is more stable, with the top and back fitted, you can turn it over to fit the plinth. A support bar for the plinth front is fitted between the sides of each base unit, screwed through the sides and biscuited to the base above it.

The plinth pieces are given an ogee moulding on the top edge with a router, cut to length, and mitred on the radial arm saw. Use a negative rake, cross-cut blade to finish and prevent 'climbing' over the work, and make adjustments with a hand plane on a shooting board.

Use biscuits in the mitres – very useful in preventing them slipping when they are clamped – apart from the obvious benefit of the extra strength.

The plinth front is fitted by screwing and gluing, from the back, on to the support bar. Apply aliphatic resin glue to the mitres for a really strong joint with no 'creep'. The first 3in (75mm) of the plinth sides are also glued to the sides, this time with PVA which allows a little movement, and clamped into position using strap and wooden hand screw clamps. The remainder of the plinth sides are left dry. They are fixed at the back, from the inside, through an oversize hole, with a screw and washer which allows for any movement in the sides across the grain.

The mitres are tapped over and sanded and finished when dry.

● TOP

The top is cut to size, the stopped housings for the sides and partition cut, allowing for a 1in (25mm) overhang all around, and the front edges rounded over to a ⅜in (10mm) radius. I prefer to fit tops upside down where possible to stop any glue running out of the housings, but this piece was too heavy to turn over on my own at this stage, without risk.

Fit the tops of the sides into the housings, and tap the top down with a rubber mallet. Clamp, and check the carcass again to see that it is still square, and then leave to set.

'The design of the cabinet started from the inside – the most important aspect, of course, was that it would take all the client's hi-fi units, cassette tapes, CDs and vinyl LPs'

● BACK

The sycamore-faced, ¼in (5mm) MDF back is cut to size, and the vent holes cut and finished with three coats of acrylic varnish. It is then glued into the pre-cut slots in the top and sides, and glued and screwed to the back edges of the shelves, drawer frames, and partition.

● PULLS

I turned a batch of pulls from brown oak for the doors and drawers. As I don't do a lot of turning I tried to standardize and repeat each action. I used sizing tools set to the relevant diameters to get them spot-on each time. Also helpful was a piece of hardboard with the profile on one side, and the positions for marking the major cuts on the other. Extras were made for matching and insurance.

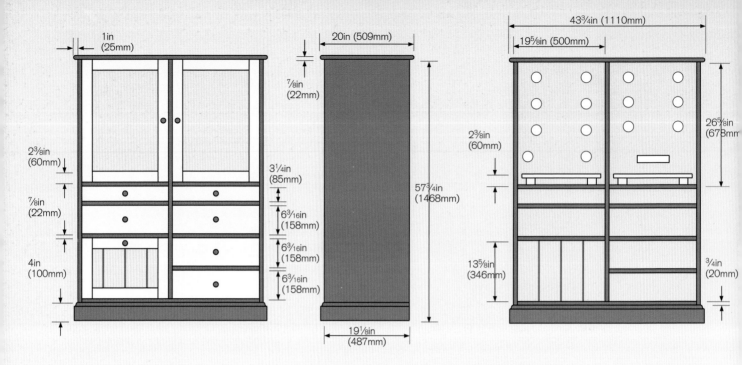

DOORS

The ripple sycamore door frame pieces are cut to size, and the top and bottom rails are joined with biscuits. Rebates are cut, with a router, on the inside of the frame, for the glass and glazing bead.

The unglazed doors are fitted in the usual way with brass butt hinges and ball catches, then removed and finished with three coats of acrylic varnish before glazing.

The ⅛in (4mm) glass is fitted into the frame on a very thin bed of clear silicone mastic, the glazing bead pinned into position, and the pins counter-sunk and filled.

DROP FLAP

The drop flap on the LP storage compartment is constructed, fitted, and finished in a similar way to the doors.

DRAWERS

The drawer fronts and casings are cut to size. The fronts are made from ⅞in (22mm) ripple sycamore, the remainder of the casings from ⅜in (10mm) oak. The bases are made from oak-faced MDF glued in all round to add strength.

The tails are cut out, under-size, on the band-saw and finished with a paring chisel. The majority of the waste for the pins is removed with a router and again finished with a sharp paring chisel. The drawers are assembled and fitted in the usual way.

COMPONENT STACK PLINTH

The component stacks have to be raised so that the door frames do not obscure the fronts. Make two shelves out of sycamore with small cylindrical feet like those on the hi-fi components. They are then ready for a finishing touch of three coats of acrylic varnish.

FINISH

The drawer fronts are finished with three coats of acrylic varnish, sanded down with 320 grit between coats. The carcass is sanded inside and out to remove any clamping or other marks, and several coats of Danish oil applied. Each coat is applied thinly, allowed to cure for 24 hours, and cut back with a Scotchbrite grey pad.

All the other finished surfaces are checked and any marks removed. Once all is clean and cured, the doors and drop flap are fitted and any minor adjustments made. Then two coats of wax are applied to the complete piece, and buffed up to a nice sheen.

CONCLUSION

This piece requires considerable and careful planning – all the measurements are critical, and I was relieved to hear that all the hi-fi equipment and music fitted!

Curvaceous

Kevin makes an oak corner
cupboard with curved doors

As more display space
was required for my wife's
china collection, we decided
on a tall cupboard with curved shelves and
doors for a corner of the dining room. The
top two-thirds were to be display shelving;
the bottom third – with doors – for storage.

⬤ DESIGN

The available space for the cupboard was measured and
the display items arranged on areas marked out to
represent the shelves; we then worked out the shelf number
and spacing. From this basic information we designed a tall,
slim, open-top unit on a chunkier bottom unit with doors.
The fronts are very narrow to give as large a display as
possible; the bottom unit a little deeper and wider than the
top unit, giving the unit extra stability. Together, with the
doors, this also gives sufficient visual weight to balance the
height of the top unit. The legs lighten its look and lift the
unit to clear the skirting board. The whole unit fully utilizes
the space available.

⬤ TIMBER

I had some nicely figured brown oak (*Quercus sp*), with
interesting colour variations and most suitable for this
piece. It had been in the workshop for some time, stored
flat with sticks between the boards. As I keep the
workshop as close to end-use conditions as possible, it
was well conditioned.

Simple and essential
corner storage

Top unit showing the
brown oak figure

Close-up of the base unit

CONSTRUCTION

CUTTING OUT

The sides and fronts would be housed directly into the top allowing a ½in (12mm) overhang; the sides fitted into the fronts in ¼ by ⅝in (6 by 16mm) housings, and the left-hand sides fitted to the right-hand sides, at the back, in a further ¼ by ⅝in (6 by 16mm) housing. The shelves are let in to the sides and fronts also in ¼ by ¾in (6 by 19mm) housings.

I draw the tops, base, and shelves to size on hardboard, and cut templates to make the marking and cutting out easier. Next, all four sides and top unit fronts are faced and thicknessed to ⅝in (16mm) then jointed to width. The tops, base, shelves and bottom unit fronts are faced and thicknessed to ¾in (19mm) and also jointed to width. Biscuits are used to strengthen the joins and prevent slippage when clamping up. The hardboard templates are also used to mark out the triangular pieces economically, with the grain direction parallel to the line of the front; this allows for movement across the grain when jointed into the sides. I made sure the best faces of the timber would be on view in the final piece.

CARCASS

The sides and shelves are cut to size; the front edges of the shelves are rounded over and the shoulder cut in where they fit into the fronts. The inside edge of the fronts of the top unit are finished nice and squarely, and at the base unit to an angle to accept the doors; the tops and bottoms are then shouldered.

The ⅝ by ¼in (16 by 6mm) housings are cut in the fronts to take the sides, and in the right-hand side at the back, to take the left-hand side. The ¾ by ¼in (19 by 6mm) housings are then cut in the sides and fronts to take the shelves. All these pieces are sanded to a finish at this point before

assembly. Next, the tops and base are cut to size and shape, and the housings for the fronts and sides cut ½in (12mm) in from the edge.

The top of the base unit also has the housing cut in its top face, to take the top unit sides. The front edges are rounded over and finished.

TOP UNIT

The top unit is dry-assembled to check the fit of all joints and adjustments made. PVA glue is applied to the housings in the fronts and sides, and the fronts, sides and shelves fitted together. To help keep the whole thing true, I dry fit the top and the top of the base unit, into which it would fit. Clamps are applied from front to back, all is checked for square and then left to set.

After the glue had set I applied PVA to the top housings, fitted it to the sides and fronts, and clamped from top to base. Again, I check all is square and left it to set. When set, I release the clamps and remove the dry fitted top of the base unit. The same sequence and procedure is used to assemble the base unit, fitting the base at the same time as the top.

LEGS

I was inspired by the leg shape from a Clarice Cliff coffee mug. The gentle curve reflected the curves on the shelves and doors, and lifted the whole piece, physically and visually. They're turned from some 3in (75mm) oak, which matched the colour of the oak I was using. A 1in (25mm) dowel is formed on the top of the legs and glued into corresponding holes in the base.

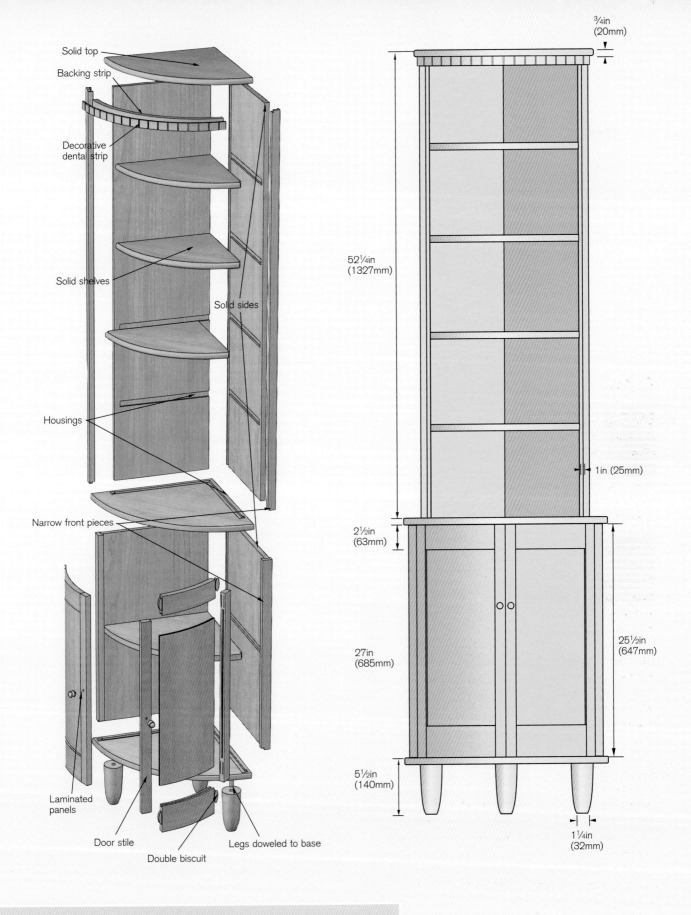

Solid top

Backing strip

Decorative
dental strip

Solid shelves

Solid sides

Housings

Narrow front pieces

Laminated
panels

Door stile

Double biscuit

Legs doweled to base

¾in
(20mm)

52¼in
(1327mm)

1in (25mm)

2½in
(63mm)

27in
(685mm)

25½in
(647mm)

5½in
(140mm)

1¼in
(32mm)

'As more display space was required for my wife's
growing china collection, we decided on a tall cupboard with
curved shelvesand doors for a corner of the dining room'

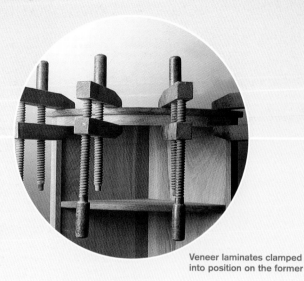

Veneer laminates clamped
into position on the former

Door frame assembly
showing biscuit joints

DECORATIVE STRIP

A backing strip is fitted to support the decorative strip under the top unit top. This is marked from the template, cut out on the bandsaw, glued and clamped to the top.

A saw cut ⅛in (3mm) deep is cut every 1in (25mm) in a strip of oak 1 by ¼in (25 by 6mm) to leave a series of small raised panels, forming the decorative strip. I mark the first cut and, using a register pencil mark on the fence of the radial arm saw, make the remaining cuts. A similar result could be achieved by hand using a tenon saw with a depth-stop clamped to the blade, or a router fitted with a ⅛in (3mm) straight cutter.

The strip is sanded, finished and cut to size, then glued into position. The kerf cuts forming the raised panels allowed the strip to follow the curve of the top.

DOOR FRAMES

I chose a double biscuit joint for the frames, thus saving an awkward mortice and tenon. The laminated curved panels are glued into the frame all round to give plenty of extra strength.

The stiles are cut to 1¼ by ⅞in (32 by 22mm) – narrow enough to avoid curving them. When in position, the side stiles are hinged to the cabinet fronts and the centre stiles sit together, thus visually doubling their width to 2½in (63mm). The top rail is cut to the same depth; the bottom rail to 3½in (90mm).

A template is cut for the curve and measurements between the cupboard fronts – effectively the plan view of the doors. From this, the rails are shaped on the bandsaw from the same oak used for the legs. They're cut too thick to allow final shaping and too long, so the ends can be trimmed to the correct angle. The end angle is taken from

Door panels

Top and bottom formers,
used to shape the door panels

The door panels are laminated from ⁵⁄₆₄in (2mm) veneers cut on the band-saw from 1in (25mm) stock, and the outside faces of this stock are sanded to a finish. The bandsaw is carefully set up with a 1in (25mm) wide, sharp, blade, and all guides and clearances checked. A supplementary deep fence is screwed to the bandsaw's existing fence and set parallel to the blade. With the finished face against the deep fence, a ³⁄₃₂in (2.5mm) sheet is cut from each side.

The freshly sawed outside faces of the thick stock are planed and sanded to a finish and two more ³⁄₃₂in (2.5mm) sheets cut. This process is repeated so I ended up with ¼ by ³⁄₃₂in (6 by 2.5mm) sheets, all finished on one side, and rough cut on the other with all with the grain running long ways.

All the veneers are are fixed to a ½in (12mm) sheet of ply with double-sided tape on the good face, and put through the thicknesser, set to 'fine', to thickness and finish the

rough-cut face. My original intention had been to make each panel from a three-sheet sandwich with the grain running vertically on the front and back faces and horizontally in the middle. This did not work – the middle sheet would not follow the curve as well as the two outside ones; so I substituted a piece of model makers 2mm, birch (*Betula sp*) -faced, three-ply – which had been lying around the workshop for years – as the centre sheet. The grain on the two outside faces of this ply ran horizontally but it followed the curve much better, which just proves you should never throw anything away!

To shape the panels I cut 'formers' from some scrap 1½in (38mm) chipboard. I select the four best veneer sheets, book matching the two front faces. Together, with the ply centre sheet, they're cut ¼in (6mm) oversize to allow for trimming. The inside faces are liberally coated with Cascamite and the sandwich clamped between the formers. Once set, they're trimmed to size and finished.

Base unit showing interior set up

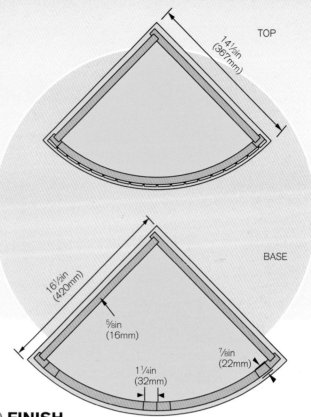

TOP

14½in (367mm)

BASE

16½in (420mm)

⅝in (16mm)

7⁄8in (22mm)

1¼in (32mm)

the template; the ends trimmed to the correct length and finally adjusted with a block plane. I ensured each door is ¼in (6mm) too wide to allow the edges to be planed to the correct angle, to fit the angled fronts inside edges. The fronts of the frames are then finished with belt and hand sanders. The biscuit slots are cut, referencing from the front of the rails and stiles, to size 10 for the top and size 20 for the bottom. The frames are dry assembled and the size of the panels measured, allowing ¼in (6mm) to be let in to a slot in the frames.

ASSEMBLY

The panels ended up slightly short of ¼in (6mm) thick, so a ¼ x ¼in (6 by 6mm) slot is cut on the inside edges of the frames to accept them. Glue is applied to the slot and all the biscuit joints, and the doors are clamped up.

Once set, the inside faces of the door frames are finished.

FITTING

I expected the fitting of the doors to be difficult but once I'd measured the angle on the hinge and opening edge, and planed it to fit, all went well. A tribute, I think, to accurate templates.

The door pulls are turned on the lathe and doweled to the door frames. I use full-length piano hinges so there was as little break to the line between the door and the front as possible.

Brass double-ball catches are fitted on the tops of the doors; I use them top and bottom when I can, but felt there might be a risk to the china from the internal fitting on the bottom shelf – and I'm not that fond of hospital food!

FINISH

Everything was hand-sanded down to 240 grit, checked carefully for marks, glue ooze etc, and wiped over with white spirit and checked again. The old oiling adage of 'once an hour for a day, once a day for a week, once a week for a month and once a year there after' is not far off. The oil was warmed, to aid penetration, and the first coat liberally applied; left to soak in and refreshed hourly until it would take no more. It was then wiped off with a soft cloth – no oil must build up on the surface – and left to harden for 24 hours in my warm workshop.

The surface was cut back with a Scotchbrite grey pad, and further light coats applied every 24 hours, and cut back with the Scotchbrite pad until the desired effect was achieved. Then a final coat of Danish oil was applied to speed up the hardening process. After a few days this last coat was cut back and buffed with a soft cloth to a sheen.

CONCLUSION

The end result was quite different from my original concept. Under the pressure of other work I resisted the complication of the curved doors but was finally won over. We all need to be jolted out of a rut occasionally – and in this case I'm very pleased I was!

Secrets &

plys 1

Make an attractive
walnut bureau with
12 secret compartments

During the UK recession of the early 1990s work was a little thin-on-the-ground, so I decided to use some of the time 'resting' between commissions to make an unusual piece; to get noticed and hopefully drum up a bit of trade.

I thought long and hard about who I was trying to impress. While, of course, I would make anything for anyone, a study of my client base revealed it was mainly middle-class, well-off couples and traditionally oriented. Also, most of my clients' contributions to design, comment, criticism and appreciation tended to come from the female side.

DESIGN

Something with visual impact, without being too far-out, which demonstrated my craftsmanship, design ability and ingenuity was required. My lady's writing desk had been very successful – as had the various multi-drawer chests.

A bit of market research – 'Come and look at my furniture designs, my dear' – and it seemed that plenty of drawers and storage compartments, in a smaller, daintier piece was the way to go. Secret compartments fascinated and intrigued me...

As well as trying to impress potential clients, I wanted a challenge to stretch me and improve my skills. An RAF colleague had retired into the antique business, where I saw a nice drop-front bureau, with a secret compartment. I hadn't made a bureau and this gave me lots of scope for drawers, storage, and secret compartments, so I decided to go down that route.

The result of my efforts is this 22 drawer, bijou bureau, with 12 secret compartments.

Front flap down, showing the small
drawers and doors for tidying desk detritus

TIMBER PREPARATION

The boule I selected contained boards of suitable dimensions and such quality there should be little wastage. The components were marked out and cut over size, sticked and left for some weeks to settle in my timber store, which has a dehumidifier. I started with the large pieces for the main carcass and drawer fronts, working down to the smaller pieces.

After the wood had settled for a couple of weeks it was faced and thicknessed, and the thin stuff for the drawer carcasses and secret compartments was deep sawn, sticked and weighted to hold it flat while it settled. This thin stuff was needed last, so it had plenty of time in the timber store while I made the main carcass.

Final conditioning of the timber takes place during the making in the workshop, which I keep warm with a stove and dry with another dehumidifier. The importance of correct conditions for timber storage and furniture making cannot be over emphasized. The closer temperature and humidity in the workshop are to the end use destination, the better.

For a piece such as this, the mechanics of the multiple drawers and secret compartments meant it was particularly important to keep any post construction movement to a minimum.

Kevin's apothecary's chest has also proved a success – it too has lots of drawers!

CONSTRUCTION

SIDES

The sides are made up first, each from two widths of walnut. The figure is matched carefully and the joint strengthened with biscuits. The edges are planed on the surfacer and finished by hand to remove the ripples. The join is made slightly hollow in the middle, so the ends are under pressure; this allows for the extra shrinkage as the end grain loses water more quickly.

The slots for the back, and stopped housings for the shelf and drawer frames, are cut in the sides with a router.

CUTTING THE SLOPE

The top of the side is drawn to full size on a piece of hardboard, to establish the position of the drop flap, hinges, and the angle of the slope. A template is made, transferred to the side, and the slope cut. The offcuts from the sides are kept to make the horns at the bottom of the slope.

An off-set shouldered tenon is then cut on each top edge to accept the top.

DRAWER FRAMES

The drawer frame fronts are made from 2 by ¾in (50 by 19mm) walnut, and the sides and backs from 50 by 19mm oak to save walnut. The backs of the frames are ¾₄in (1mm) longer than the fronts to make the frames – and therefore the assembled carcass – ¾₄in (1mm) wider at the back. This gives a little clearance as the drawers are pushed home, for easy movement. The drawer spacers are tapered front to back, by a tiny bit each side, for the same reason.

Mortices were cut in the frame fronts and backs and tenons formed on the sides. The frames are assembled with the front joints glued, but the back joints left dry, with an expansion gap, to allow for movement in the carcass sides.

The diagonals are measured, adjustments made to square up the frames, and they are left to set. The diagonals are shouldered front and back to go into the stopped housings in the sides.

The front uprights, between the drawers, are cut to size and a ¼in (6mm) shouldered tenon cut on each end. Corresponding mortices are cut in the frames, and the drawer spacers fitted. The lopers are treated as drawers with uprights and spacers fitted to locate them.

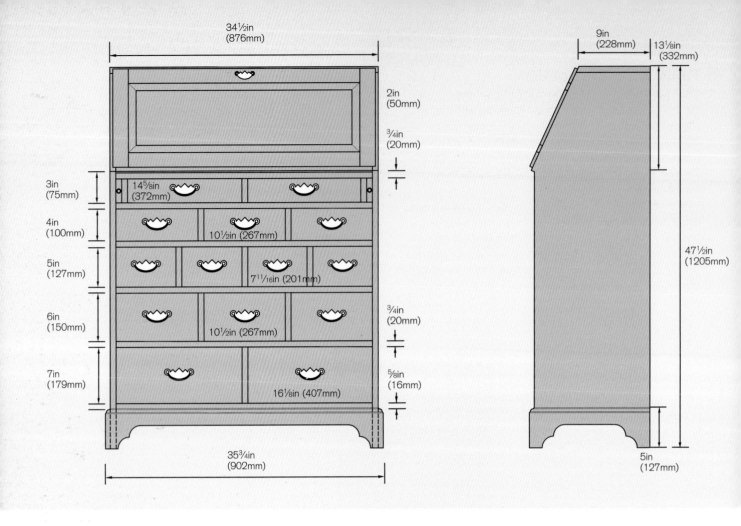

34½in
(876mm)

2in
(50mm)

¾in
(20mm)

3in
(75mm)

14⅝in
(372mm)

4in
(100mm)

10½in (267mm)

5in
(127mm)

7¹¹⁄₁₆in (201mm)

6in
(150mm)

10½in (267mm)

¾in
(20mm)

7in
(179mm)

16⅛in (407mm)

⅝in
(16mm)

35¾in
(902mm)

9in
(228mm)

13⅛in
(332mm)

47½in
(1205mm)

5in
(127mm)

'Biscuits are used in the mitres –
very useful in preventing them
slipping when they're clamped up –
apart from the obvious benefit of
the extra strength'

CARCASS ASSEMBLY

The initial carcass assembly required careful preparation because of the large number of joints to be glued and clamped at the same time.

All the pieces are finished as far as possible, and then check fitted dry. The clamps and equipment were all ready with plenty of time allowed – this was not a 'Friday afternoon' job.

The drawer frames are glued into the sides, and the uprights glued between the rails. Only the front and back rail ends of the frames should be glued into the side slots, so the dry joint at the back can run smoothly.

The back and front diagonals of the carcass are checked to ensure all is square and the carcass is then left to set.

PLINTH

A support bar for the plinth front is fitted between the sides, screwed through the sides and biscuited to the base above it. The plinth pieces are given an ogee moulding on the top edge with a router, cut to length, and mitred on the radial arm saw. I use a negative rake cross-cut blade for finish and prevention of 'climbing' over the work; adjustments are made by hand on a shooting board.

Biscuits are used in the mitres – very useful in preventing them slipping when they're clamped up – apart from the obvious benefit of the extra strength.

The sides of the plinth are offered up to the ends of the carcass sides and the cut-out shape marked with a pencil. The ends of the carcass sides are then cut out with a jigsaw to correspond with the cut-out in the plinth. The plinth front is fitted by screwing and gluing, from the back, on to the support bar. Aliphatic resin glue is applied to the mitres, for a really strong joint with no 'creep'. The first 2in (50mm) of the plinth sides are also glued to the sides, this time with PVA, which allows a little movement, and clamped into position. The remainder of the plinth sides are left dry; they're fixed at the back, from the inside, through an oversize hole, with a screw and washer. This allows for any movement in the sides, across the grain.

The mitres are tapped over, where necessary, and sanded when dry.

Walnut is a delight to work, and the favourite of many a cabinetmaker

Engraved escutcheons and handles

Doors open revealing yet more drawers

Drawer divisions, runners, stops and kickers

Timber selection

English and French, Italian or Turkish, and so on, are all European walnut (*Juglans regia*) and are named according to region. The various regional types vary in colour, figure and texture but all have typical characteristics.

English walnut – the king of timbers – was my choice for this piece. It works easily, is stable, polishes to a high finish, and smells lovely when cut. Unfortunately, it was also very difficult to find in sufficient quantity and quality. English walnut trees tend to be older and larger than European, with good figure and some ripple, making them highly prized – and priced – for veneer production. In the end I had to settle for steamed French walnut. This timber is very similar to English walnut but generally in smaller boards. It is steamed to reduce

the colour contrast between the dark heartwood and the light sapwood, enabling the sapwood to be used in construction. The steaming process makes the wood even easier to work and the sawn logs are treated with an insecticide to reduce the sapwood vulnerability to insect attack.

At my timber yard it was sold in complete boules, with the boards bound together sequentially. Once I had chosen a likely looking parcel – of about the right total volume and dimensions – I opened it up to have a good look at all the faces of all the boards. This timber was expensive and so I didn't want any unpleasant surprises!

Traditionally dovetailed, of course

The top of the loper is felt
covered to protect the front flap

'English walnut trees tend to be older and larger than European, with good figure and some ripple, making them highly prized – and priced – for veneer production'

⬤ STANDARD DRAWERS

All the pieces for the drawers are cut to size, fitted and marked. The fronts from ⅞in (22mm) walnut, the carcasses from ¼in (6mm) oak, and the bases from ³⁄₁₆in (5mm) oak-faced MDF. The thin drawer carcasses give a lightness and look of quality.

The sides are slotted for the bases, taped together in double pairs, with the top one marked out, and the pins cut on the bandsaw.

Holes are drilled in the fronts for the handles. Then the fronts and backs are marked one at a time from the pins, and the majority of the waste removed with a router. Each joint is then individually finished with a sharp chisel; the drawer assembled, with the MDF base glued in all round, and pinned at the back, checked for square and wind, then left to set.

The open back of the carcass made the final fitting of the drawers relatively easy. The extra ³⁄₆₄in (1mm) of space at the back, created by the taper on the drawer frames and spacers, also helped and they all ran freely. They are clearly marked on the back to identify their position.

In the next section, Kevin completes the project and talks you through the false components and those tantalizing secret drawers.

Secrets &
plys 2

The two deepest drawers are given a false base 1½in (38mm) higher than the normal position, and glued into position. A second base is put in the correct position but not glued in, so it could run in and out in the slot. A secret drawer is constructed on this second base. The back of the main drawer is split with the top section fixed into position by the usual dovetails. The bottom section becomes the front of the secret drawer.

The join line is hand planed to a tight and inconspicuous fit. The bottom of this secret drawer front extends into the side as a dry comb joint approximating a dovetail. The only indications of the false base are the depth of the drawer, not obvious if full, and the join line on the back.

In the second part of his walnut bureau project, **Kevin** outlines the drawers and reveals some of those 12 secret compartments

The drop flap is frame-and-panel construction

● SHORT DRAWERS

The line of three 6in (152mm) drawers is made 2in (50mm) shorter than the others to allow a secret compartment behind them. This is a simple false back, matching the real back, held in place by standard magnetic catches. Removing the drawer above, or below, gives access to the top or bottom edge.

The many-drawered desk

Eight drawers on the inside,
how many more secret ones?

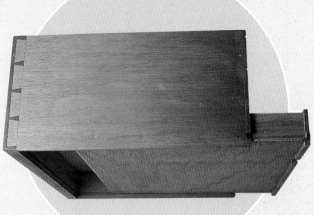

The two larger drawers
have false bottoms

Drop-front

The corners of the frame are morticed and tenoned and a shouldered rebate cut to accept the front solid floating panel and the backing ply panel to carry the leather top. The frame front edges are stop chamfered on the router and finished with a scraper. The outside edges of the frame sides and top are rebated ½ by ½in (13 by 13mm) to allow it to inset into the carcass sides and top.

The front panel is formed from a deep-sawn, bookmatched piece of walnut. The centre join is strengthened with biscuits, taking care to place them so they would not be exposed when the panel was fielded. The fielding is done on the router table, with a vertical cutter on a big router, and finished with a scraper and a sanding block. This panel is finished and dropped into the front deeper, narrower rebate in the frame.

A ply panel is cut to size to fit in the wider, shallower rebates; its top edge about ⅟₁₆in (1.5mm) below the back face of the frame. This is glued and pinned to the frame to hold the front panel in place, strengthen the frame, and provide a stable, flat surface for the leather skiver.

The flap hinges are positioned on the back edge of the frame and scribed round with a scalpel. A router with a straight-plunge cutter, set to the correct depth, is used to remove the majority of the waste, and the edges are finished with a chisel.

The frame is offered up to the bureau shelf, the hinge positions marked, and the rebates on the shelf cut the same way.

The hinges are screwed into position, slots all lined up, and the front's drop-movement checked.

With the front in position, the size and shape of the hornes at the bottom of the front slope are marked. The hornes are cut from the pieces of scrap removed from the sides to form the slope, and glued into position.

The lock rebate is routed into the top of the frame inside face in a similar way to the hinges. The keyhole is drilled and chiselled out, and the escutcheon fitted to the front face. The drop front is closed and the dead bolt from the lock shot with the key, several times, to leave a mark on the inside face of the top of the carcass. A recess is cut at that mark to receive the lock bolt, to lock the drop front.

LOPERS

The lopers to support the drop flap are cut to size, fitted, and the front face edges chamfered. They're inserted from the open back, between the uprights. Stops are fitted on the inside edges to engage the back of the front inside, upright. I decided not to have an automatic lever system to open the lopers; it can look ugly and out of place and might have got in the way of the secret compartments.

After the final finishing, the tops of the lopers will be covered with green baize to protect the finish on the drop flap.

BRASSWARE

All the brassware is chosen from Savill's catalogue. I found some unusual engraved plate-drop handles for the drawers, with a matching escutcheon for the flap lock. The tiny drops for the lopers – and the pulls for the internal drawers and doors – are also similarly engraved. They're all in antiqued brass and this provided some extra detail.

SIDE VIEW SHOWING FALSE BACK

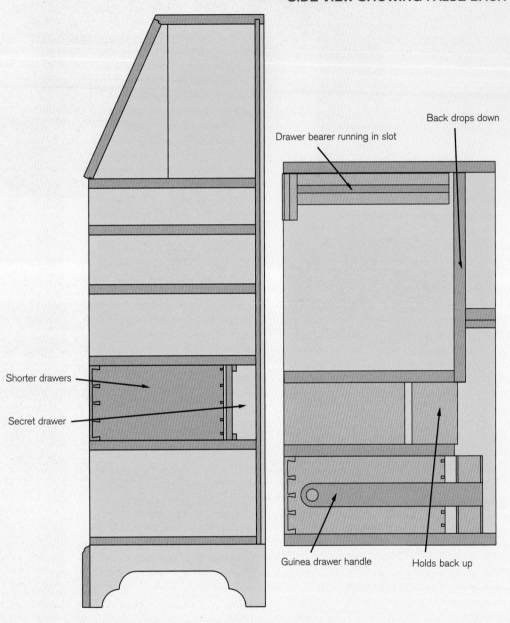

Drawer bearer running in slot

Back drops down

Shorter drawers

Secret drawer

Guinea drawer handle

Holds back up

⬤ TOP INSET

With the main carcass top, drop front, and back not yet
fitted I began the top inset. From the drawing you can see
this is made from a mirrored right and left side, joined
together with shelves and a front with doors. The two side
carcasses are made first, including secret compartment
work, then glued into position. The shelves are fitted
between, all hidden work completed. Drawers and doors
are fitted from the front.

⬤ SIDE COMPARTMENTS

Both side compartments are made up from ⅜in (10mm)
walnut (Juglans sp) joined with stopped housings, top and
bottom off-set inwards. Screws or dowels can be used, as
the outer faces will not be seen. The eight small standard
drawers are constructed in the same way as the main
drawers; six have brass pulls and the two behind the doors
have a finger pull cut out. The doors are morticed and
tenoned frames with floating, fielded panels. One has a
small, brass bolt inside and both have the same brass pulls
as the drawers.

70 | Furniture Workshop

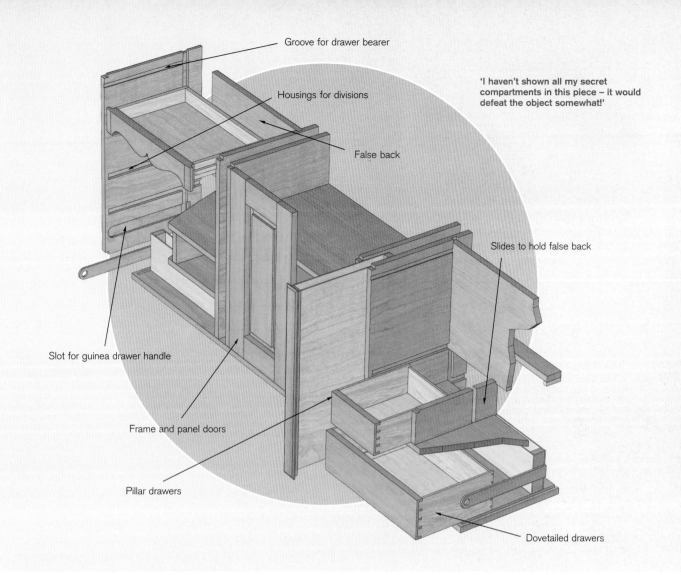

Groove for drawer bearer

Housings for divisions

False back

'I haven't shown all my secret compartments in this piece – it would defeat the object somewhat!'

Slides to hold false back

Slot for guinea drawer handle

Frame and panel doors

Pillar drawers

Dovetailed drawers

SECRET COMPARTMENTS

False backs and sides are put in, and a number of secret compartments constructed, differing in the means of access. Not all false back space is used for secret compartments and this can be very frustrating for a searcher!

The frieze or stamp drawer is common to both, but with completely different methods of locking closed, so a casual attempt gives no indication they open. Both pillar drawers are spring loaded from the back and have different release mechanisms. On the right-hand side, one of the hinge screws for the door is longer than the others, located in the side of the drawer, and is turned to release the drawer which then springs out. The other drawer has a different release catch.

On the insets either side, the false backs drop down when the back half of the divider – between the two drawers – is slid towards the front. It drops as far as the ball catch at the base. Only when clicked past that catch can the false bottom be opened, and the container therein removed. A secret compartment within a secret compartment!

The guinea drawer – used to hold stacks of guinea coins in the past – on this side was a straight copy from the antique bureau I had seen, with a slender handle inset into the carcass side, running past the drawer in front of it. The centre and right-hand compartments also have a number of secret compartments – which I'll leave to your imagination.

SMALL CONTAINERS

I made good use of $\frac{1}{16}$in (1.5mm) modelling three-ply in the construction of the containers for the secret compartments. It's light, strong, maximizes the space, and is available from modelling shops.

The pillar drawers are made with a $\frac{3}{8}$in (10mm) solid back, front and base, with modelling ply sides glued on. The guinea drawer has solid ends and base, with the same ply used for the back and front. The container under the false bottom at the back of the left hand side is similarly constructed.

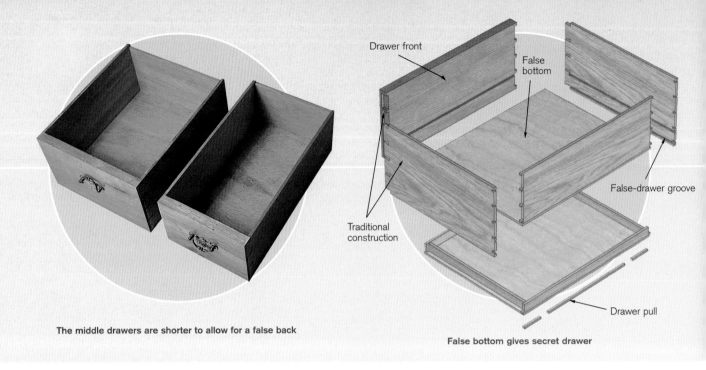

The middle drawers are shorter to allow for a false back

Drawer front

False bottom

Traditional construction

False-drawer groove

Drawer pull

False bottom gives secret drawer

SECRET SECRETS

I haven't shown all my secret compartments in this piece – it would defeat the object somewhat! I hope what I have shown gives food for thought and enables readers to apply their own ingenuity to the project.

The principles to remember are disguise, tailoring the compartment to the secret, and ingenuity of access. Remember that once fitted it's difficult to adjust many of the moving components, particularly the sliding ones. Make sure the wood has stabilized, and adjusted to the end-use conditions. I also used hard candle wax to lubricate everything, as an added precaution. Most secret compartments can be discovered by a determined searcher with a ruler and a torch. Of course, 12 are only to show off – I'm a man, so I haven't got 12 secrets to keep!

TOP

Once the top insets have been completed, fit the top of the carcass. This is cut to size and the front edge planed to the slope of the sides, for the drop front to close onto. A stopped housing is cut on the underside at the back to take the tops of the oak-face MDF back, and on each end to take the tenon on the top of the sides. On reflection I don't much like this join from the sides to the top, and would with hindsight prefer a biscuited mitre or through dovetails. Fortunately, the exposed end grain polished up very well and looks quite decorative, if a little clumsy.

The top is glued and clamped into position; I check carefully there's no distortion caused to the carcass via the clamping for fear of its effect on the many moving parts.

BACK

When sure no further adjustments are required, I fit the back. It's a single piece of ³⁄₁₆in (5mm) oak-faced MDF, cut to fit into the slots already cut, in the sides and top. Glue is applied to the slots and backs of the back main drawer rails. The back is sprung into the side slots and I slide the last ¼in (6mm) into the top. It's then pinned to the drawer rails. This back arrangement provided a lot of rigidity but was a bit heroic. Pinned tongue and groove boards would not give the rigidity but do give easy access to the false backs if necessary.

FINISH

All the surfaces had been power-sanded down to 150 grit during the making. All are re-checked for glue, marks or blemishes, and hand-sanded down to 320 grit. Properly prepared, walnut oils to a beautiful finish, so I decided on that. To retain tradition I used linseed oil – the boiled variety – which dries a little faster. The essence of oiling is to make sure the oil is absorbed into the wood and does not build up on the surface. 'Little' and 'often' are the watchwords. It helps if the oil is warm – to reduce viscosity and aid penetration – and the finishing area is warm and dry to aid drying and curing.

Warm the oil by standing the container in very hot water and apply thin coats, working it in well with a soft, clean, lint-free cloth. When I was sure it was well covered and would absorb no more, the excess was wiped off with kitchen tissue, and the surface buffed with another soft

Probably safer than under the mattress!

A guinea drawer is revealed, the handle is recessed in the carcass side

clean cloth. This process is repeated every 24 hours for a week or so until a really nice finish is achieved. I then gave it a thin final coat of Danish oil to aid curing and left it for a week in my warm dry workshop. It was then moved into the house and left to stand for another two weeks. Tests and adjustments are completed, and the final assembly commenced.

FINAL ASSEMBLY

A leather skiver with tooled edges was ordered from a specialist supplier. I cut it to size and glued it to the ply back of the drop front, with heavy duty wallpaper paste. This has good initial tack and still allows some sliding into position. I worked from the middle to the outside edges, rubbing gently but firmly with a soft cloth, to remove air bubbles, and flatten the leather into position, being careful not to stretch it. Once it had dried I did the final trimming to the edges of the ply panel with a scalpel.

All that remained was to fit the handles, escutcheon, pulls, and the baize strips to the tops of the lopers. These completed, the bureau is pronounced fit for action!

CONCLUSION

I enjoyed making this piece and it certainly achieved my aim for publicity. I prepared a press release and got into all the local papers. The local television news team visited and did a 20 minute slot, touring my cottage and covering my work in general, culminating with the bureau. A video tape of that interview has been left in one of the secret compartments. A competition was run in a local department store, at that time displaying some of my work, to see if anyone could find all the secret compartments – that needed careful policing!

So, plenty of publicity but did it result in any orders? I did get several orders which could be traced to it, including a complete dining room in steamed French walnut (*Juglans regia*).

We still have the bureau. My wife, Yvonne, loved it so much I gave it to her as a consolation prize when she married me in 1994!

Make a Morris chair

Based on an original by William Morris, this chair has been interpreted in many ways over the years. It even featured in early American mail-order catalogues as a bare-wood flatpack, for home assembly and finishing!
I saw one of these chairs at furniture-maker Guy Butcher's workshop and he said he had made it from plans in a book on the American Arts and Crafts movement.
At the time my wife and I were looking for something other than a standard three-piece suite for our cottage. I quickly realized that the chair could be interpreted as a sofa and a rocker, giving ample scope for individuality.

Kevin tackles an Arts and Crafts classic that crossed the Atlantic

Derived from a Morris design, this chair proved to be popular in America

DESIGN

The American plans gave measurements for a version which was, to say the least, generously proportioned. I completely re-scaled it to fit our sitting room. It also had the seat upholstered to a drop-in frame, with a reversible loose cushion back. We decided to web the drop-in frame and keep the reversible loose cushion seat. The post through tenons on the chair I had seen were proud of the arm's top face by ¼in (6mm), which was visually pleasing but would, I felt, result in large quantities of alcohol and glass ending up on the floor! I decided to make them flush.

SELECTING THE TIMBER

The standard timber for such a chair would be oak. In fact the period mail-order catalogue entries made much of the fact that it was 'quarter-sawn' oak to boot. I wonder if that would mean much to the average catalogue shopper today? The destination room has large areas of oak in the floor and exposed beams, as well as pieces in elm, burr elm, and

Close up of the through-tenon in the arm

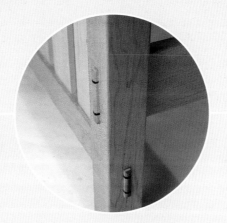

Wedged through-tenons on the rails

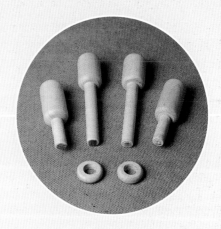

The finished pivot and adjustment pegs

walnut. We like to mix different types of wood for variety. My 'artistic director' decided she wanted something darker than sycamore, lighter than cherry, and without the pronounced figure of the English oak. We eventually settled on American hard maple.

PREPARING THE MAPLE

I bought the maple from my local joinery supplier. The advantage of using American timber is that it is more readily available and of more consistent quality and price than native timbers. It is also available in straight-edged, long, boards and in a wide range of thicknesses, helping to reduce wastage. I was, for instance, able to buy a 2½in (63mm) rather than 3in (75mm) thick board to get the posts out of.

The timber had, however, been kiln-dried in America before shipping, and transported and stored in unknown conditions for an unknown time. I treated it as air-dried and conditioned it thoroughly in my wood store, with its dehumidifier, for several weeks before use.

My workshop is kept at a temperature to replicate end-use conditions, so conditioning continued throughout the making.

CONSTRUCTION

The sequence of construction was to make the sides, join them together to make the base, add the back frame, drop in the seat frame and finally add the loose cushions.

MAKING THE SIDES

I cut the leg posts to size, and cut the through-mortices for the rails. I used my planer morticing attachment for this and squared them off with a chisel. While squaring the ends, I made the mortice a little wider at the front so the wedges would splay the through-tenon and make a dovetail shape. This also makes it easier to assemble the mortice and

tenons. I drilled the posts for the back pivot pins, and radiused all edges, other than the top, to ⅛in (3mm) with a router. The legs I marked front and back, left and right.

RAILS

Next I cut the rails to size and the tenons, which would protrude ¼in (6mm) proud through the legs, formed on the ends. I routed out the tenon cheeks on the router table, and cut the shoulders on the bandsaw. I cut the tenons a tiny bit tight, and finally adjusted them using a bench hook and shoulder plane, until they were a push fit. I also made saw cuts for the wedges on the bandsaw. Contrasting wedges were made from some walnut off-cuts. The top and bottom edges of the rails were also radiused to ⅛in (3mm).

ARMS

I cut the arms to size, and drilled them to take the back adjusting pegs. I marked the through-mortices to take the post tenons with a scalpel, and routed out the bulk of the waste freehand on the router table, then finished by hand with a 1½in (38mm) chisel. I then cut the end taper and finished the end grain with a block plane, and radiused the top and bottom edges to ⅛in (3mm).

Marking through-tenons on the arms

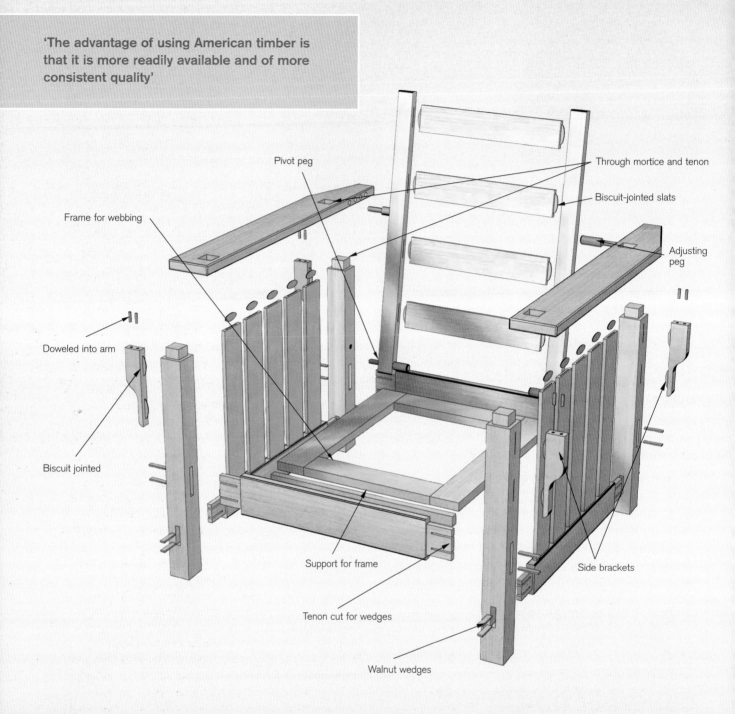

Pivot peg

Frame for webbing

Through mortice and tenon

Biscuit-jointed slats

Adjusting peg

Doweled into arm

Biscuit jointed

Support for frame

Side brackets

Tenon cut for wedges

Walnut wedges

American hard maple

American hard maple (Acer saccharum), also known as rock maple, is a cream to pale straw-coloured, strong, close-grained timber, with fine brown lines giving a nice gentle emphasis to the figure. Sometimes it has a ripple effect, like sycamore. Hard to work, it blunts tools and can chip easily.

It takes a good natural finish but stains unevenly. Very resistant to wear, it is used in flooring, pianos, shoemakers' lasts, and for textile, dairy, and laundry machinery. It should not be confused with soft maple, which is soft, pinkish and streaked.

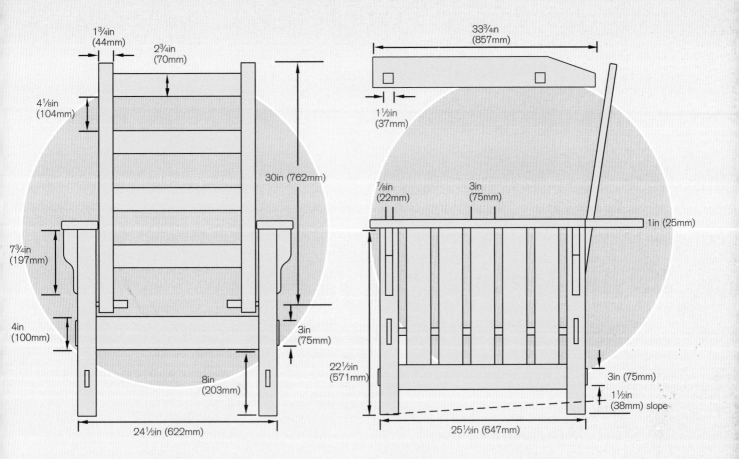

POST THROUGH TENONS

Next I chocked the arm and relevant leg and clamped them into position on the bench. Using the finished arm through mortices, I marked the tenons on the top of the legs with a scalpel. I made the cross-cuts for the tenon shoulders on the radial arm saw, removing the bulk of the waste on the bandsaw, and finishing the tenons to a tight fit by chisel and shoulder plane. I cut the tenons to protrude through by a very small amount so that I could sand them flush later.

SIDE SLATS

Next came the slats. I faced and thicknessed the slats to ½in (13mm), cut to length, and slotted top and bottom for biscuits. The underside of the arms and the top edge of the side rails were also slotted for biscuits, and the slats check fitted. Biscuits are perfectly suited to this application, saving a huge amount of time over mortice and tenons.

SIDE BRACKETS

I cut the brackets to size and shaped them on the bandsaw, sanded radiused the outside edges to ⅛in (3mm). Then I dry-assembled the sides (without the slats), and marked the biscuit positions. The top of the bracket was doweled to the underside of the arm.

ASSEMBLING THE SIDES

I sanded all the parts for the sides on the belt and orbital sanders and check fitted them. I assembled the various clamps required and adjusted them to size, before finally hand sanding the parts to 240 grit.

The arm was dry fitted to the top of the posts and glue applied to the mortice and tenon, and the saw cuts and wedges of the side rail. The side rail was clamped into position and the wedges knocked home. The side was checked square and left to set.

The arm was then gently tapped off, glue applied to the post tenons and arm mortices, and all the slat biscuits and slots. I fitted it all together briskly, tapped it home with my trusty rubber mallet, as necessary, clamped it up, and checked it was square. Once set, the brackets were glued up, fitted and clamped into position.

When I'd assembled both sides and they were set, I marked the cut from the front face of the front leg to the back face of the back leg and cut it on the bandsaw to produce the rake of the chair. I planed and sanded the post tenons flush with the arms.

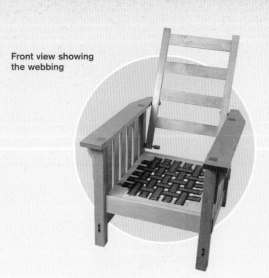

Front view showing
the webbing

Side view showing
sloped angle of the chair

BASE ASSEMBLY

The complete base is formed by joining the two sides with the front and back rails. First I applied glue to the mortices, tenons, wedges, and saw cuts. Then I tapped the tenons through, knocked home the wedges and applied clamps. I stood the base on my flat assembly area, checked it for square and wind, and left it to set.

THROUGH-TENON FINISHING

The end grain of all the rail through-tenons was finished with a block plane, Then I cut a piece of hardboard to place on the face of the leg, with a slot to fit over the tenon stubs and chamfered the edges with a shoulder plane.

BACK FRAME

I cut the back frame stiles to size, radiused all edges to ⅛in (3mm) and drilled the ends for the pivot pins. I cut the slats to size and cut biscuit slots in the slats and the stiles. Finally I power- and hand-sanded all the pieces, dry-fitted, glued and clamped them up.

PINS

I turned the pivot and adjustment pegs on the lathe – accuracy ensured with my trusty sizing tool! Then I turned wooden spacer washers blind on the lathe, and drilled the hole out on the pillar drill.

SEAT FRAME

This was a simple frame which should be of hardwood, better to take the upholstery nails. I used double biscuits for the corner joints. The seat frame sits on battens screwed and glued to the front and back rails.

UPHOLSTERY

Joan Milton, who specializes in DIY upholstery supplies, kindly gave us some very helpful advice on the sort of foam and webbing to use. I webbed the seat frame with elasticated webbing and she provided the correct grade of foam, cut to size, for me to have simple box cushions made locally.

FINISH

We tried various finishes to get the right effect and finally decided on Liberon finishing oil, which I prefer, as it is more penetrative and gives less colour change than some other Danish oils.

I checked everything for glue ooze, and hand-sanded the chair down to 320 grit. Several coats of oil were applied in the usual way and the chair left for a few days in my warm workshop to fully cure before use. Finally I fitted self-adhesive felt buttons to the bottom of the legs to protect the wooden floor.

THE FINAL RESULT

The scaling was successful, as the chair does not need to be any bigger for normal use. The detail of the ⅛in (3mm) radiusing on most of the edges gives a nice soft effect and making the through tenons on the arms flush is essential!

Let's rock

Project 5 Project

This chair was to be part of a seating set comprising a fireside chair, a sofa and this rocker. The aim was to produce a flexible seating arrangement without resorting to a standard three-piece suite. Some aspects of the project are common to all three pieces and are repeated for convenience.

With more than a nod to the Arts and Crafts movement, **Kevin** makes a Morris-style rocking chair

DESIGNED TO ROCK

The fundamental change to this version of the chair was to add rockers. Even though the fireside chair had been scaled down from the original American measurements, there was also still scope to reduce the seat size even further.

The through-tenons in the arms and legs of the fireside version increased the making time considerably, so we decided to use blind tenons on this version. This allowed the side rails to be brought up, level with the seat rails, and the side slats shortened to fit. The side slats were also reduced in width, and increased in number, to further lighten the look. The end result was a chair which was obviously linked in form and style to the fireside chair, with sufficient difference in the detail to add interest. It's a 'Mummy' version of the 'Daddy' chair!

TIMBER SELECTION

The standard timber for such a chair would be oak, but the room this chair is destined for has large areas of oak in the floor and exposed beams. It also has pieces in elm, burr elm, and walnut, as we like a mix of woods for variety. My wife decided she wanted something darker than sycamore, lighter than cherry, and without the pronounced figure of the English oak. After a lot of discussion we settled on American hard maple (Acer saccharum). This is a cream to pale straw-coloured, strong, close-grained timber, with fine

'Ley' back and gently rock

Attractive ripple figure on the arm

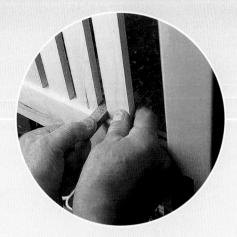
Spacer for accurately positioning the side slats

brown lines giving a nice gentle emphasis to the figure. Some has a ripple effect, like sycamore, and I found some very nice ripple in the order and saved it for the arms of this chair.

The wood is hard to work, blunts tools, and can chip easily. It takes a good natural finish with a smooth, silky feel, but stains unevenly. Very resistant to wear, it is used in flooring, pianos, shoemakers' lasts, and textile, dairy and laundry machinery. It should not be confused with soft maple, which is soft, pinkish and streaked.

TIMBER PREPARATION

The advantage of using American timber is that it is, paradoxically, probably more readily available and of more consistent quality and price than some native timbers. It is also available in straight-edged, long boards and a wide range of thicknesses, helping to reduce wastage. I was able to buy a 2⅛in- rather than 3in-thick board for the leg posts,

from my local timber merchant and local joinery supplier. The timber had, however, been kiln-dried in America before shipping, and transported and stored in unknown conditions for an unknown time. I treated it as air-dried and conditioned it thoroughly in my wood store, with its dehumidifier, for a several weeks before use. The workshop was kept, as usual, at end-use conditions, so that conditioning continued throughout the making.

CONSTRUCTION

The sequence of construction is to make the sides, join them together to make the base, add the back frame, fix the rockers, drop in the seat frame and add the loose cushions.

Turning the pegs

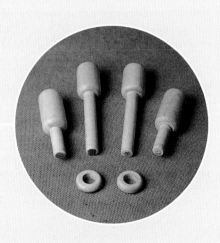
The finished pegs and spacers

Fitting the blind dowel on the leg-to-arm joint

'The 'in-use' angle
for the chair can be adjusted
by altering the position of the
chair along the rockers,
before fixing'

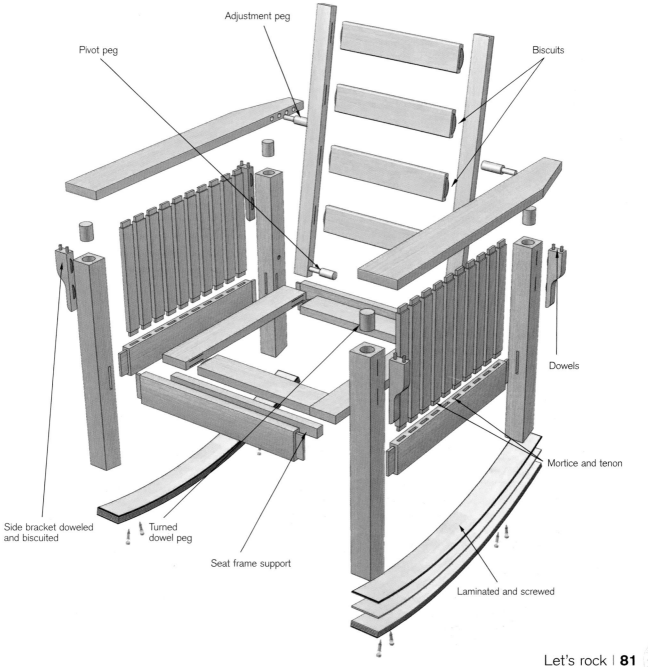

Adjustment peg

Pivot peg

Biscuits

Dowels

Mortice and tenon

Side bracket doweled
and biscuited

Turned
dowel peg

Seat frame support

Laminated and screwed

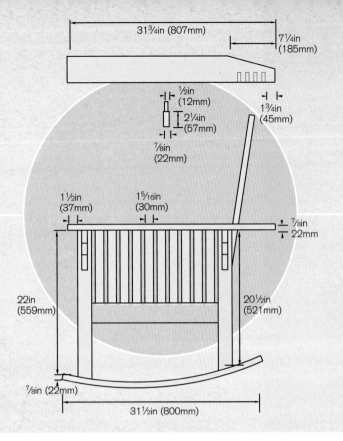

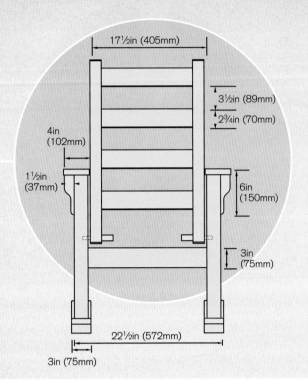

MAKING THE SIDES

LEG POSTS

The leg posts were cut to size, allowing 1in (25mm) over-length, and the blind mortices cut for the rails. These were cut on my planer morticing attachment and squared off with a chisel. The posts were drilled for the back pivot pins, and all edges, other than the top, radiused to ⅛in (3mm) with a router. The dowel pin on the top of each leg to attach it to the arm, were turned on the lathe, using my trusty sizing tool and bedan for an exact fit. The legs were carefully marked front and back, left and right.

RAILS

Next the rails were cut to size and the tenons formed on the ends. The tenon cheeks were made by multiple cuts on the radial arm saw and the shoulders on the bandsaw. The tenons were cut full, and finally adjusted using a bench hook and shoulder plane, until they were a push-fit. The top and bottom edges of the rails were also radiused to ⅛in (3mm).

ARMS

I cut the arms to size and drilled them to take the back adjusting pegs. Blind holes were drilled to take the post dowels. The corner was cut off the outside edge of the back end of each arm, to form the end taper. All the end grain of the arms which was finished with a block plane, and the top and bottom edges were radiused to ⅛in (3mm).

SIDE SLATS

The slats were faced and thicknessed to ½in (13mm), cut to length, and a short tenon formed top and bottom, again on the radial arm and bandsaws. The underside of the arms were morticed with a router and the slats check fitted.

Unfortunately biscuits could not be used here as the slats are too narrow.

SIDE BRACKETS

The brackets were cut to size and shaped on the bandsaw, and belt sander, and the outside edges radiused to ⅛in (3mm). The sides were dry-assembled (without the slats) and the biscuit positions to fit the side brackets were marked and cut. Holes were drilled in the top of the bracket and the underside of the arm, to take the fixing dowels.

ASSEMBLING THE SIDES

All the parts for the sides were sanded on the belt and orbital sanders and checked for fit. The various clamps required were assembled and adjusted to size, and the parts were finally hand-sanded to 240-grit.

The arm was dry-fitted to the top of the posts and glue applied to the mortice and tenon of the side rail. The side rail was clamped into position. The side was checked square and left to set.

The arm was then gently tapped off, glue applied to the post dowels and arm blind holes, and all the slat mortice and tenons. All was briskly fitted together, using a piece of

Rockers

The rockers were made of laminated strips of maple, which were cut 1in (25mm) over-length, ⅛in (3mm) thick, on the bandsaw. One side was faced on the planer, before cutting from the source piece. I cut extra pieces as insurance in case of accidents during thicknessing.

Before thicknessing, each strip was fixed to a piece of ¾in (19mm) MDF with double-sided carpet tape, and a fine cut set on the thicknesser. Very thin strips are likely to shatter if put through a thicknesser without a backing, and most thicknesser tables won't go that close to the knives – fortunately!

To form the curve of the rockers I made up a simple jig from ply. The strips were well coated with Titebond and clamped up with sash clamps, then a G-clamp was used at each end to stop the strips sliding out of place during the clamping up.

Once set, the rockers were trimmed to length and the edges were finished with a hand plane. The front and back edges were 'nosed' by rounding over with a ⅜in (10mm) radius bit in the router.

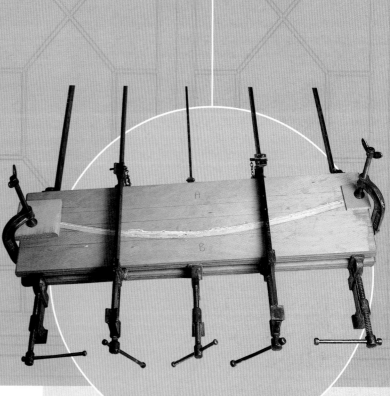

Laminates for the rocker sleds glued up in the jig

ply to check the spacing of the slats, tapped home with my trusty rubber mallet as necessary, clamped up, and checked square. Once set, the side brackets, dowels and biscuits were glued, fitted, and the brackets clamped into position.

ASSEMBLING THE BASE

The complete base is formed by joining the two sides with the front and back seat rails. Glue was applied to the mortices and tenons, and clamps applied. The base was stood on my flat assembly area, checked for square and wind, and left to set. My assembly area is an 8 x 4ft piece of 1 in MDF on the floor of the workshop which has been set true with a spirit level to ensure pieces stand vertical!

FITTING ROCKERS

The base of the chair was laid on its side, the finished rockers were placed on the side of the legs, in the correct position and the line of the cut required on the legs, marked. This slant cut was made by hand, and repeated for the other side.

The chair base was then turned upside-down and screws were driven through the rockers into the legs. They were driven at an angle, to form a dovetail shape, countersunk into the underside of the rockers, and the countersunk holes plugged with a piece of maple.

Cutting tenon cheeks on radial arm saw

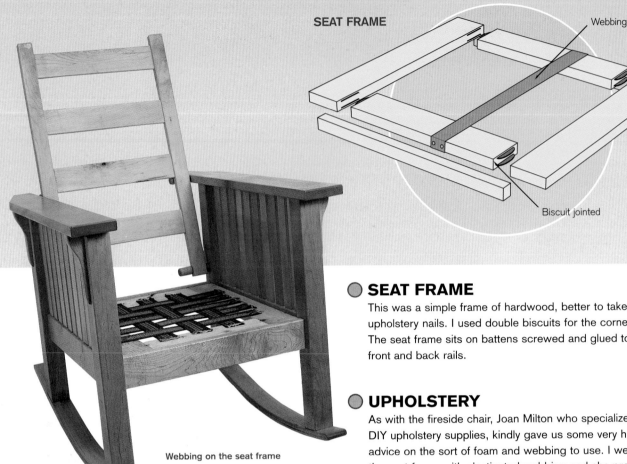

Webbing

Biscuit jointed

Webbing on the seat frame

The 'in-use' angle for the chair, can be adjusted by altering the position of the chair along the rockers, before fixing. There must be a body seated in the correct, comfortable, position in the chair when this is done, to achieve the correct centre of gravity. The 'at rest' position of the empty chair may be different.

BACK FRAME

The back frame stiles were cut to size, all edges radiused to ⅛in (3mm) and the ends drilled for the pivot pins. The slats were cut to size and biscuit slots cut in the slats and the stiles. All the pieces were power-sanded and hand-sanded, dry-fitted, glued and clamped up.

PINS

Pivot and adjustment pins were turned on the lathe, again accuracy ensured with my trusty sizing tool! The wooden spacer washers were turned blind on the lathe, and then the hole drilled out on the pillar drill.

SEAT FRAME

This was a simple frame of hardwood, better to take the upholstery nails. I used double biscuits for the corner joints. The seat frame sits on battens screwed and glued to the front and back rails.

UPHOLSTERY

As with the fireside chair, Joan Milton who specializes in DIY upholstery supplies, kindly gave us some very helpful advice on the sort of foam and webbing to use. I webbed the seat frame with elasticated webbing and she provided the correct grade of foam, cut to size, for me to have simple box cushions made locally. We decided to have these cushions covered in the same natural, hand-woven, cotton as the fireside chair, but in a different colour.

FINISH

As with the previous piece, this one was also finished with Liberon finishing oil which I prefer to some other Danish oils, as it is more penetrative and gives less colour change.

Everything was checked for glue ooze, and hand-sanded down to 320-grit. Several coats of oil were applied in the usual way and the chair left for a few days in my warm workshop to fully cure.

The soothing rocking motion of this chair makes it very popular, and even with the further scaling down it is quite big enough for most adults. The figure and ripple on the arms are a particularly attractive feature.

Sofa

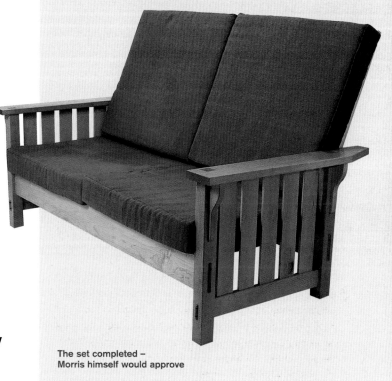

so good

Project 6 Project

This sofa completes the Morris-style seating set I made for our cottage. The aim was to produce a period seating arrangement suitable for a cottage, but a bit more individual than a standard three-piece suite.

The fireside chair is covered on pages 74–78, and the rocker on pages 79–84. Some aspects of the project are common to all three pieces and are repeated here for convenience.

We decided to base the sofa on the fireside chair rather than the rocker, because the latter's original American design measurements had been scaled down even further than the chair.

The sofa was to retain all the detail of the chair, essentially being a 'stretched' three-seater version.

As the front and back rails have a much greater span and carry the seat frames, they were beefed up to cope. The sides were essentially the same as the chair, with the arms widened slightly to keep in proportion to the increased width, and the side brackets were suitably scaled up. The rails on the back had 'noggins' added between them to stiffen the back.

Having made the chair, I now fully appreciated the extra time involved in making the through tenons, and was all for going for the blind tenons I had used on the rocker. But my design consultant – Yvonne –

A three-piece suite's sofa is more than just a stretched fireside chair, as **Kevin** explains

The set completed – Morris himself would approve

felt that the detail provided was essential to the overall look. Easy for her to say – but I was, of course, over-ruled!

The post-through tenons on the arms were kept flush as on the chair, and for the same reasons. In order to emphasize the link to the chair we used the same colour of natural hand-woven cotton for the covers.

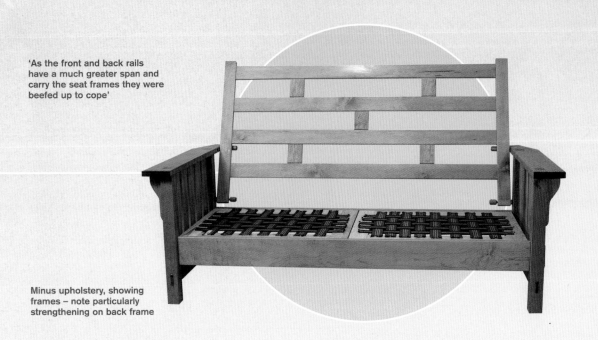

'As the front and back rails have a much greater span and carry the seat frames they were beefed up to cope'

Minus upholstery, showing frames – note particularly strengthening on back frame

TIMBER PREPARATION

I made the chair in maple purchased in the UK from Kidderminster Timberworld, part of the Arnold Laver group of Timberworld merchants and my local joinery supplier. The advantage of using American timber is that it is, paradoxically, probably more readily available and of more consistent quality and price than many native timbers.

It is also available in straight-edged, long boards and a wide range of thicknesses, helping to reduce wastage. I was, for instance, able to buy a 2½in- rather than 3in- thick board for the posts.

The timber had, however, been kiln dried in America before shipping, and transported and stored in unknown conditions for an unknown time. I treated it as air-dried and conditioned it thoroughly in my dehumidified wood store for a several weeks before use.

The workshop was kept, as usual, as warm and dry as the room in which the furniture would end up, so that conditioning continued throughout the making.

CONSTRUCTION

The sequence of construction was to make the sides first, join them together to make the base, and add the back frame. The seat frames and box cushions were added last, after the finish had cured.

SIDES

The leg posts were cut to size, and the through mortices cut for the rails using my planer morticing attachment. They were squared off with a chisel. While squaring the corners I made the mortice a little wider at the front so that the

wedges would splay the through tenon and make a dovetail shape. This also makes it easier to assemble the joints.

The posts were drilled for the back pivot pins, and all edges other than the top radiused to ⅛in (3mm) with a router. The legs were carefully marked front and back, left and right.

RAILS

The rails were cut to size and the tenons, which would protrude ¼in (5mm) proud through the legs, formed on the ends. The tenon cheeks were routed out on the router table, and the shoulders cut on the band saw.

The tenons were cut a little tight on the saw, and finally adjusted with a shoulder plane on a bench hook. Saw cuts for the wedges were also made on the bandsaw. Contrasting wedges were made from some walnut offcuts, and the top and bottom edges of the rails were also radiused to ⅛in (3mm).

ARMS

The arms were cut to size, and drilled to take the back adjusting pegs. The through mortices to take the post tenons were marked with a scalpel, the bulk of the waste being routed out on the router table using the fence for the sides and free hand for the rest.

They were finished by hand with a 1⅛in chisel. The end taper was then cut, the end grain finished with a block plane, and the top and bottom edges radiused to ⅛in (3mm).

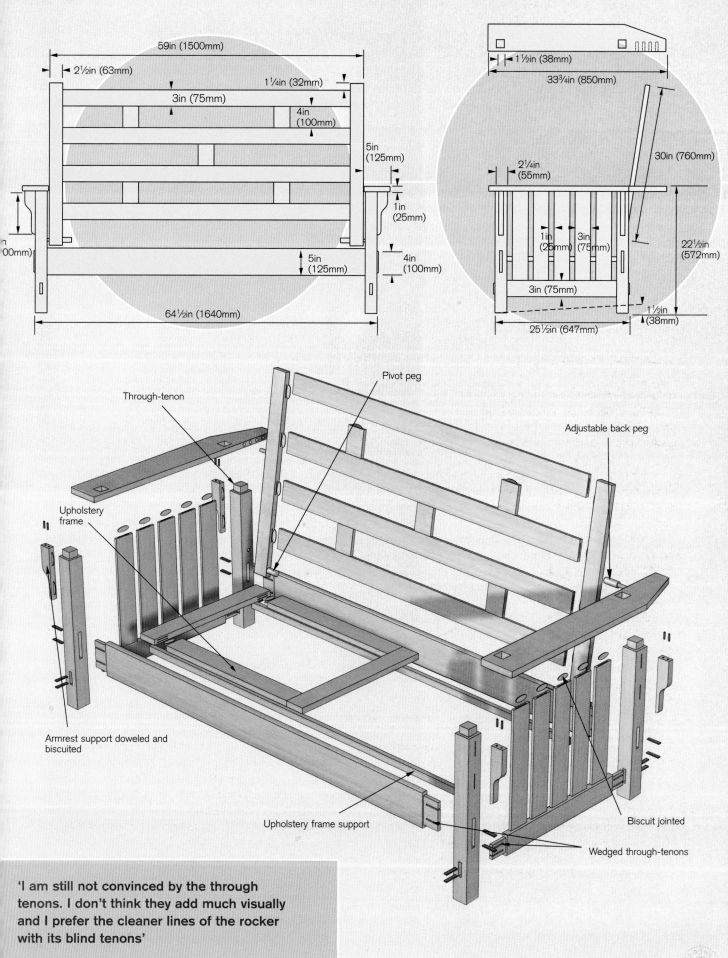

59in (1500mm)

2½in (63mm)

1¼in (32mm)

3in (75mm)

4in (100mm)

5in (125mm)

1in (25mm)

5in (125mm)

4in (100mm)

64½in (1640mm)

00mm)

1½in (38mm)

33¾in (850mm)

2¼in (55mm)

30in (760mm)

1in (25mm)

3in (75mm)

22½in (572mm)

3in (75mm)

1½in (38mm)

25½in (647mm)

Through-tenon

Pivot peg

Adjustable back peg

Upholstery frame

Armrest support doweled and biscuited

Upholstery frame support

Biscuit jointed

Wedged through-tenons

'I am still not convinced by the through tenons. I don't think they add much visually and I prefer the cleaner lines of the rocker with its blind tenons'

Knifing across the mortices

Squaring off the slot cut mortices

Routing tenon cheeks

Timber selection

The standard timber for the Morris chair was quarter-sawn oak. In fact some of the period mail order catalogue entries made much of the fact that the leg posts were veneered on two sides to give the flash and figure of the medullary rays on all four sides. A nice detail I suppose, but perhaps over egging the custard?

Our sitting room has large areas of oak in the floor and exposed beams, as well as other furniture pieces in elm, burr elm, and walnut, as we like to mix woods for variety. We began looking for something darker than sycamore, lighter than elm, without the pronounced figure of the English oak, and capable of a good smooth finish; American hard maple fitted the bill. This is a cream to pale straw-coloured, strong, close-grained timber, with fine, brown lines giving a nice gentle emphasis to the figure. Some has a ripple effect like sycamore.

Hard to work, it blunts tools and can chip easily. It takes a good natural finish but stains unevenly. Very resistant to wear, it is used in flooring, pianos, lasts, and textile, dairy, and laundry machinery. It should not be confused with soft maple which is soft, pinkish and streaked.

⬤ POST THROUGH-TENONS

The arm and relevant leg were chocked and clamped into position on the bench and the tenons on the top of the legs were marked with a scalpel, using the finished arm through mortices as a guide.

The cross cuts for the tenon shoulders were cut on the radial arm saw, the bulk of the waste removed on the bandsaw, and the tenons finished to a tight fit by chisel and shoulder plane.They were allowed to protrude through by a very small amount which would be sanded flush. Wedges were not used on these tenons, as I felt they were too short to splay. The end grain was very close and I sealed it thoroughly to prevent shrinkage. So far – one year later – this has been 100% successful.

⬤ SIDE SLATS

The slats were faced and thicknessed to ½in (13mm), cut to length, and slotted top and bottom for biscuits. The underside of the arms and the top edge of the side rails were also slotted for biscuits, and the slats check fitted. Biscuits are perfectly suited to this application and save a huge amount of time over mortice and tenons.

⬤ SIDE BRACKETS

The brackets were cut to size and shaped on the bandsaw, sanded and the outside edges radiused to ⅛in (3mm). The sides were dry-assembled – without the slats – and the biscuit positions for the brackets marked. The tops of the brackets were doweled to the underside of the arm.

⬤ ASSEMBLING THE SIDES

All the parts for the sides were sanded on the belt and orbital sanders and check fitted.

The various clamps required were assembled and adjusted to size, and the parts finally hand-sanded to 240 grit. The arm was dry-fitted to the top of the posts and glue applied to the mortice and tenon, and the saw cuts and wedges of the side rail. The side rail was clamped into position and the wedges knocked home. The side was checked square and left to set.

The arm was then gently tapped off, glue applied to the post tenons and arm mortices, and the slat biscuits and slots.

This was all briskly fitted together, tapped home with my trusty rubber mallet as necessary, clamped up, and checked square.

Once set the brackets were glued up, fitted and clamped into position.

When both sides had been assembled and were set, the cut from the front face of the front leg to the back face of the back leg was marked and cut on the band saw to produce the rake. The post tenons were planed and sanded flush with the arms.

BASE ASSEMBLY

The complete base is formed by joining the two sides to the front-and-back rails. Glue was applied to the mortices, tenons, wedges, and saw cuts. The tenons were tapped through, the wedges knocked home and clamps applied. The base was stood on my flat assembly area, checked for square and wind, and left to set.

THROUGH-TENON FINISHING

The end grain of all the rail through tenons was finished with a block plane, and the edges with a shoulder plane. A piece of hardboard with a slot to fit over the tenon stubs can be used to avoid marking the leg.

BACK FRAME

The back frame stiles were cut to size, all edges radiused to ⅛in (3mm) and the ends drilled for the pivot pins. The slats and noggins were cut to size, the sides radiused to ⅛in (3mm), and the biscuit slots cut. All the pieces were power and hand-sanded, dry-fitted, glued and clamped up.

PEGS, PIVOTS, SPACERS

Pivots and adjustment pegs were turned on the lathe, accuracy being ensured with a sizing tool! The wooden spacer washers were turned blind on the lathe, and then the hole drilled out on the pillar drill.

SEAT FRAME

This was a simple frame which should be of hardwood because it has to take the upholstery nails. I used double biscuits for the corner joints. The seat frame sits on battens screwed and glued to the front and back rails.

UPHOLSTERY

Joan Milton, who specializes in DIY upholstery supplies, kindly gave us some very helpful advice. I webbed the seat frame with elasticated webbing and she provided the correct grade of foam for the seats and backs, cut to size. I could then have simple box cushions made locally.

FINISH

As with the chairs, the sofa was also finished with Liberon finishing oil, which I prefer, as it seems more penetrative and gives less colour change than some other Danish oils.

Everything was checked for glue ooze, and hand-sanded down to 320-grit. We had a spell of nice weather so the sofa was oiled – and I was Guinness-ed – in the shade of the cherry tree in the garden. Both of us clean, dry, and slightly oiled!

Several light coats of oil were applied, left to cure for 24 hours, and cut back with a Scotchbrite grey pad between coats. The sofa was left for a few days to fully cure before use. Finally, self-adhesive felt buttons were fitted to the bottom of the legs to protect the floor.

COTTAGE COMFORTS

The sofa is comfortable and suits our requirements well. We are pleased with the function and visual effect of the whole seating arrangement; it's a little different and is, we feel, nicely in keeping with our cottage.

I am still not convinced by the through tenons. I don't think they add much visually and I prefer the cleaner lines of the rocker with its blind tenons.

I would be sure to warn any client of the increased cost they incur. Just because something is technically difficult to do it does not necessarily improve a piece.

A Cumbrian coffer

I have a client who lives in a lovely old cottage in a beautiful rural village. She has a real appreciation of individual pieces of furniture and she first saw my work in an exhibition at Barnard Castle, in the north of England. Since then, I have made many pieces for her and her family.

I had made a 14-drawer apothecary's chest and a smaller three-drawer chest, both in wych elm (*Ulmus glabra*) and English elm (*Ulmus procera*) burr. Both pieces ended up being housed in a small reading room in her cottage, which was liberally sprinkled with African artefacts, from her close association with Zimbabwe. She had loved the rich texture, wild figuring and warm colouring of the burr and elm, as it complemented the general ethnic flavour of the room.

Kevin makes a small burr elm chest

● TIMBER SELECTION

The choice of timber had already been made to fit in with the other pieces, but it is worth mentioning a little about elm and burr elm.

Elm can vary considerably in colour, texture, figure and stability, depending on which of the sub species it is. English elm is the darkest with the wildest grain and the most figure, and as a result, the least stable. Dutch elm (*Ulmus hollandica*) is lighter and more stable, with straighter grain and less figure. Wych elm is even straighter grained, paler in colour, often with a green streak, and the most stable of the three.

DESIGN

The small chest that I had been commissioned to make was to store magazines. My client was adamant that it could be easily moved around the room, so we decided to put it hidden castors. The size was dictated by the space available for the finished chest and the standard dimensions of a magazine.

The client had seen a much bigger coffer chest in English elm and burr in my cottage and liked its frame and fielded panel construction. She preferred the gentle contrast of wych elm for the carcass of her piece and fortunately, I still had some in stock, left over from previous projects.

The frames and panels would be joined without post legs, allowing the castors to be recessed inside the resulting hollow corner. We decided that a solid top was more suitable as this would enable the chest to be used as an occasional side table.

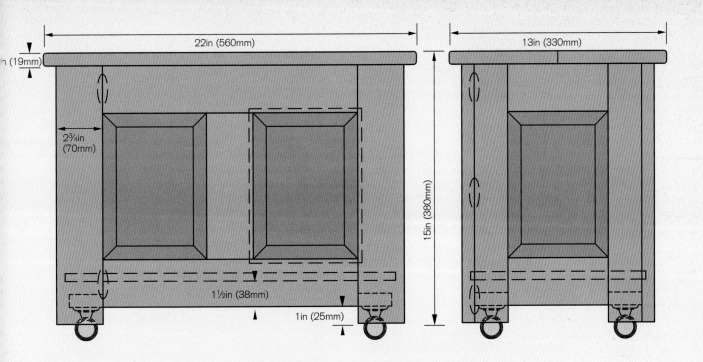

All three types are affected by Dutch elm disease although there are still reasonable supplies of the timber available in the UK, mainly in the North. It is currently being replanted in the South where the disease has run its course.

Burr elm is mainly from isolated hedgerow trees. It is often not commercially viable to timber merchants, and frequently ends up being sold as logs. It is worth harvesting, but, having decided some time ago that I am a furniture-maker and not a timber merchant, my days of roaming remote places with the chainsaw, and protracted negotiations with farmers, are firmly in the past. Now my log supplier brings it to me – in exchange for money, of course!

Larger pieces are planked at a local sawmill, while smaller pieces can be done on my bandsaw. It is stick-dried in my wood store and finished, if necessary, in my small home-made conditioning cabinet.

The main problem with all burr is wild grain – live and dead knots of all sizes, in-growing bark, cracks, blemishes, that type of thing. It can be very hard and quite soft all in the same board. Humidity has a serious effect as it takes in and gives up water relatively easily, causing movement.

Careful seasoning and selection of the wood, sharp tools, adequate tolerances and a thoroughly sealing finish are all required to get the best out of this timber. Finishing can also give a marked change from the dry colour and it is well worth giving it a coat of white spirit to get a temporary idea of the likely final colour.

CONSTRUCTION

The frame and floating panel construction allows for the inevitable movement in the burr panels, which were small enough to be cut in one piece. This piece seemed to be ideally suited to biscuit construction. Make no mistake – if traditional makers had had biscuit jointers and modern glues, they would have certainly used them where appropriate. I decided to make double joints, for maximum strength.

FRAMES

The rails and stiles for the frames were cut to size from the wych elm, while the edges and ends were planed exactly square, and checked for a perfect fit on the joints.

The positions for the biscuit slots were marked exactly in the centre of the relevant ends and transferred to the correct sides.

With the jointer set, the first level of slots were cut ¼in (6mm) down to their centre. Once this had been done and checked carefully, the depth setting was reset to cut ½in (13mm) down to the centre of the second slot.

Another way would be to mark the joints on both sides and use the same depth setting from each side. The method I used is quicker, but it is obviously important to double-check that you have made all the first cuts before you change the depth setting.

HOUSING SLOTS

At this point the housing slots for the panels were cut, taking care to stop them, where appropriate, in the relevant frame pieces. Some of these slots cut slightly into the biscuit joints, but these could be trimmed with a paring chisel after the frames had been dry assembled and the size of the panels, including the overhang locating into the housing slots, measured.

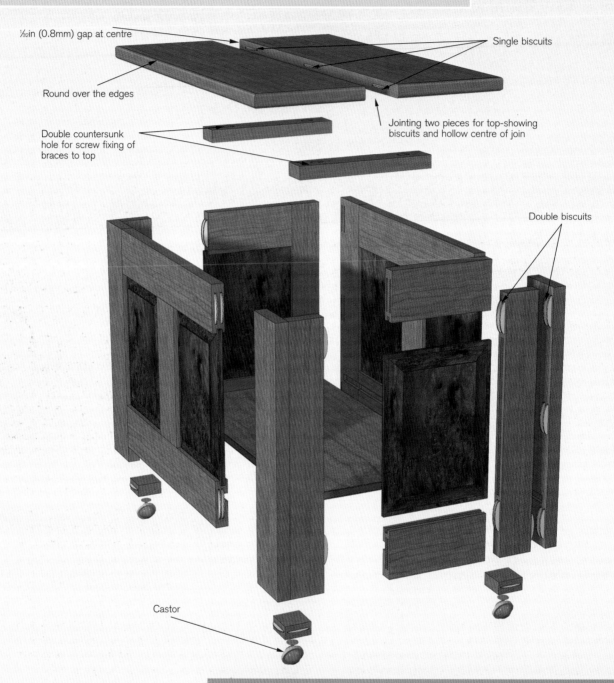

1/32in (0.8mm) gap at centre

Round over the edges

Single biscuits

Double countersunk hole for screw fixing of braces to top

Jointing two pieces for top-showing biscuits and hollow centre of join

Double biscuits

Castor

Timber preparation

All this timber had been in my wood store for some years where it was sticked and stacked to settle and condition in a dehumidified environment. Once the pieces selected for this project were cut out, generously oversize, they were restacked on sticks in the warm, dry, workshop, enabling drying and settling to be continued evenly during the making. The tops of the stacks were weighted to hold the timber flat, and it was kept like this throughout the making, except when actually being worked on. Not a bad habit to get into during a project – especially if it is left for any length of time.

Exploded front/back panel showing biscuits

Top view of 'exploded' chest

Carcass assembly

The frames were carefully belt-sanded to 150 grit. On the front and back frames the centre stile was sanded first, followed by the top and bottom rails, and then the outer stiles. On the side frames the sequence was top and bottom rails, then stiles. Belt sanding in this order ensures that the final pass removes any cross-grain scratching. After belt sanding, the frames were sanded to a 150-grit finish with a random orbital sander, which can be used across the grain without scratching. It would be possible to do the whole job with a random orbital sander, starting with a coarse grit, although this would take longer. The completed frames were

to be butt-joined together, with biscuit reinforcements, to make the chest carcass. The edges were planed true, the biscuit slots cut, and the joints check-fitted dry. The clamps were set to size and the cauls were prepared. Titebond was applied to the biscuits, slots, frame edges, and base housing slot. Everything was assembled together, clamped, checked for square and wind, and left on a level floor to cure.

Once cured, the carcass was up-ended, and the castor blocks put into place with the help of some glue and a biscuit jointer. The castors were positioned so that the chest just cleared the floor allowing for some 'sink' into the carpet.

⬤ PANELS

The burr panels were cut to size and belt-sanded down to 150 grit. The majority of waste for the fieldings was removed using a vertical cutter on my friend the T9, that was fitted to a router table. This was done in a series of shallow passes to leave a pretty good finish. To get the corners exactly how I wanted them, I used a sharp shoulder plane to make a line from the corner of the raised centre to the outside corner of the panel.

Finally, the panels were sanded to a finish and given a coat of oil which was left to cure for 24 hours. This was to colour the edges inside the housing slot in case they were exposed by shrinkage.

⬤ ASSEMBLY OF THE FRAMES

Titebond glue was applied to the biscuits and slots, the panels were dropped into place, and the frames, which should be clamped up, were measured across the diagonals, adjusted to ensure they were square, and then left to set.

Once set, the housing slot for the base was cut, stopped on the front and back frames. This slot was set high enough for the blocks which would be set into the hollow corners to take the castors.

⬤ BASE

The base was made from cedar-of-Lebanon-faced MDF to match the drawers on the chests I had previously made. I prefer sheet materials for bases such as this, as they can be glued all round into the housing slot, giving great strength for little weight and volume.

⬤ TOP

The top was made from two pieces that were butt-jointed together with reinforcing biscuits. A planer was used to straighten and square the edges, followed by a hand plane to remove the ripples. The edges were left slightly hollow in the centre, to ensure the ends pulled up tight when

The completed coffer

A small cod chest
made for the same client

A previous larger coffer chest, for a different client,
with internal trays made from cedar of Lebanon

clamped. This also allowed for a little extra shrinkage at the ends, which dry out more through the end grain.

Titebond was applied to the edges, biscuits, and slots and the top was clamped up, checked to ensure there was no wind, and left to set. Once set the top and bottom edges were rounded over with a ⅜in radius cutter on the T5.

Braces were put across the top to keep it flat, with plugged screws in double countersunk holes. The double countersinking allows for movement of the wood across the grain without cracking, while the screws hold the top flat to the braces.

The top was fitted to the carcass with a piano hinge and adjusted to fit all round when closed. The overhang at the back allows it to go just past the vertical to stay open.

FINISH

I don't think you can beat an oiled finish for elm or burr – it shows off the wonderful rich colour and figure in the wood and seals and stabilises it at the same time. The satin finish masks any slight but inevitable blemishes in the surface of the burr. I prefer Liberon finishing oil which penetrates well and cures quickly without getting sticky during application. The whole piece was checked carefully for any marks, blemishes, and glue ooze, and then hand-sanded down to 240 grit.

The first coat of oil is the most important, as once it has cured, very little further penetration takes place. I kept the first coat wet all day by frequently refreshing it with more oil,

until no more could be soaked up by the relatively porous wood. After that all the surplus oil was removed with kitchen roll and the chest left to dry for 24 hours in my warm, dry workshop.

A further light coat of oil was applied every 24 hours for the next week, rubbing down between coats with a Scotchbrite grey pad, making sure there was no build up of oil on the surface.

The other advantages of using an oiled finish are that it is easily renewed with a small drink, and, like so many of us, improves with age and a bit of TLC.

CONCLUSION

While on a trip we delivered the chest to my client who had kindly invited my wife and I to lunch. It was a very enjoyable visit and my client was pleased with the chest. I was flattered to learn that she keeps any articles about me or the pieces I have made for her. She says she wants future generations to know who was responsible! So, with that in mind, this book is a lasting one for the archives, which I guess will be housed in her coffer. Now that's very apt!

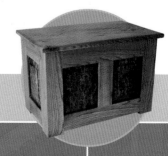

Light

sleeper

Project 8 · Project

Our home was completely furnished with a range of my pieces, giving me the scope to practise techniques and ideas and show different woods and designs in situ. I also found this lived-in showroom an invaluable and cost-effective selling device.

When we sold the house the purchaser bought a lot of the furniture, including our king-sized bed. However, after a short period of sleeping on a mattress on the floor in our new cottage, my wife Yvonne indicated quite firmly that it would be a good idea for me to make another bed for us. I heard and obeyed!

Kevin makes a stunning king-sized bed from light ash to go in his new home

King-sized for the Queen!

⦿ TUCKING IN

We decided on a simple, traditional design with a slatted base to take the king-sized mattress, which we had kept. The exact mattress size is important and should be measured first. I allowed ½in (13mm) clearance on the length to tuck in the duvet at the foot, and ¼in (6mm) on the width to allow for under sheets or a blanket. These allowances are not critical as the mattress will compress between the head and foot and between the sides of the slatted base. A greater allowance may be required for a bed made up with lots of blankets, rather than a duvet.

The size of a bed like this demands that it be knock-down for ease of transport and access. This design was easily made as three pieces – head, foot, and base.

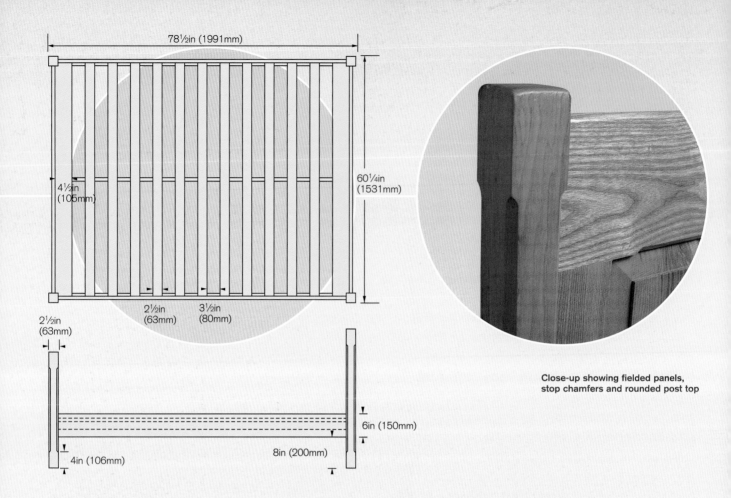

78½in (1991mm)

4½in
(105mm)

60¼in
(1531mm)

2½in
(63mm)

3½in
(80mm)

2½in
(63mm)

6in (150mm)

4in (106mm)

8in (200mm)

**Close-up showing fielded panels,
stop chamfers and rounded post top**

The head and foot are easily manoeuvred up stairs and through doorways, and the base can, if necessary, be broken down even further to the individual sides and slats. The whole thing is simple to assemble in its final resting place – praise the Lord, and pass the power screwdriver!

⬤ SOFT OPTIONS

We wanted a light timber with some interesting figure for the furniture in this bedroom, and the bed was only the start. Bedside chests of drawers, and a large free-standing wardrobe would come later. Such big pieces would crowd the room and steal the light if made from a dark wood.

The bed we had left behind was made of English ash and had quite a lot of brown and olive streaking in it. We wanted more of a white ash with a small amount of the brown and olive colour for interest. I had some suitable English ash in stock, and it was pretty well ready to work having been in the dehumidified wood store for some time.

To make quite sure the timber was ready, I wanted to let it adjust to the conditions in its final destination and there was plenty of space in the bedroom as we had no furniture. So I cut the whole lot out, suitably oversize to allow for final dimensioning, and left it there, sticked, for a couple of weeks. As usual my workshop was kept warm and dry during the making so that the wood continued to condition throughout.

CONSTRUCTION

The sequence of construction was to make the head and foot, join them with the sides and drop in the slats and centre support.

⬤ HEAD AND FOOT

The top and bottom rails of the head and foot frames were cut to size and the mortices for the upright stiles cut. Next, the stiles were cut to size and the end tenons formed, slightly over-size, on the bandsaw. They were adjusted with a shoulder plane to fit the mortices. The rails and stiles were stop chamfered with a bearing guided chamfer cutter, on the router table.

A slot was cut in the inside edges of the frame stiles and rails to accept the fielded panels, using a light router with a side fence, leaving the chamfer cutter set up on the table to do the leg posts.

The legs were cut to size and also stop chamfered. All the stop chamfers were then cleaned up with a sharp cabinet scraper and block sanded to a finish.

The panels for the head and foot were made up from deep-cut, book-matched pieces of brown-and-olive-streaked ash, edge jointed and reinforced with biscuits.

The fieldings were formed by a number of shallow cuts, using a vertical profile cutter on the router table. They were

'My workshop was kept warm and dry
during the making so that the wood continued
to condition throughout'

PANELS

The panels for the head and foot were made up from
deep-cut, book-matched pieces of brown-and-olive-
streaked ash, edge jointed and reinforced with biscuits.
The fieldings were formed by a number of shallow cuts,
using a vertical profile cutter on the router table. They
were finished with a shoulder plane and scraper where
necessary, followed by a light sanding. The front and
back faces of the panels were belt and orbital sanded
down to 120-grit. A groove was cut in the inside edges
of the frame stiles and rails to accept the fielded panels,
using a light router with a side fence, leaving the chamfer
cutter set up on the table to do the leg posts.

HEAD AND FOOTBOARD

The top and bottom rails of the head
and foot frames were cut to size
and the mortices for the upright stiles
cut. Next, the stiles were cut to size
and the end tenons formed, slightly
over size, on the bandsaw. They were
adjusted with a shoulder plane to fit the
mortices. The rails and stiles were stop
chamfered with a bearing guided
chamfer cutter, on the router table.
The legs were cut to size and also stop
chamfered. All the stop chamfers were
then cleaned up with a sharp cabinet
scraper and block-sanded to a finish.

SIDE RAILS

The side rails were cut to length and the 2in-deep tenon formed on each end,
again on the bandsaw, and planed to a running fit in the leg post mortices. The
top edge was rounded over to match the head and foot frame top rails. The side
rails were slotted in to the leg mortices and the bed was clamped up. It was all
checked for square and the pilot holes for the fixing screws were drilled, and
counter sunk, on the insides of the legs. An alternative method, if you don't
mind the screw heads showing, would be to fix from the outside.

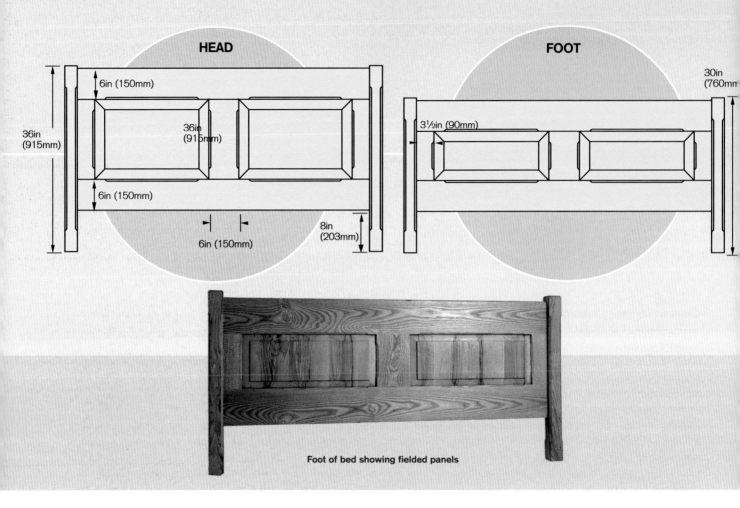

HEAD

6in (150mm)

36in (915mm)

36in (915mm)

6in (150mm)

6in (150mm)

8in (203mm)

FOOT

30in (760mm)

3½in (90mm)

Foot of bed showing fielded panels

finished with a shoulder plane and scraper where necessary, followed by a light sanding. The front and back faces of the panels were belt and orbital sanded to 120-grit.

FRAME TESTS

All the pieces of the head and foot frames were test fitted dry, and the inside edges hand planed and sanded. PVA glue was applied to the mortice and tenons, and the frames assembled, with the panels in place, clamped, checked for square and wind, adjusted as necessary and left to set.

When they had set the shallow tenons were formed on the sides of the frames using the light router with a side fence. The corresponding mortices were cut in the legs with the same router. A mortice was cut in the centre of the inside faces of the head and foot frame bottom rails to take the ash centre support rail for the slats.

The top edges of the top rails of the frames were finished with a hand plane and rounded over using a bearing guided ¼in radius cutter, and the frames belt and orbital sanded down to 120-grit.

The edges of the tops and bottoms of the legs were also rounded over with the same cutter. The legs were deep morticed for the bed sides, belt and orbital sanded down to 120-grit, and glued and clamped up on to the frames, with packing to protect the finish on the legs.

SIDE RAILS

The side rails were cut to length and the 2in (50mm) deep tenon formed on each end, again on the bandsaw, and planed to a running fit in the leg post mortices.

The top edge was rounded over to match the head and foot frame top rails. The side rails were slotted in to the leg mortises and the bed was clamped up. It was all checked for square and the pilot holes for the fixing screws were drilled, and counter sunk, on the insides of the legs. The screws were driven home and the clamps removed.

The 2½ x ⅞in (63 x 22mm) ash slats were cut to length, ½in (12mm) short, allowing clearance between the slat ends and the side rails, to avoid any squeaking of the bed caused by movement! A bearer rail of 2 x ⅞in (50 x 22mm) ash was glued and screwed to the inside of the bed base, 2in (50mm) below the top of the rails, on the sides, head and foot, to support the slats and screw them on to. The centre support rail was cut to size, tenons formed and fitted into the mortices in the head and foot bottom rails. The tops of the slats were 1⅛in (30mm) below the top edges of the sides, forming a recess to drop the mattress into. Finally, spacer blocks, to be glued and pinned on the side bearer rails between the slats, were required, which needed to be individually cut.

Repetitive injury

Repeat-cutting a large number of small items, like the spacer blocks for use between the slats, can become mindless and, sure enough, on about number 17 my brain became disengaged, with the result that the bandsaw blade snuck up on my blind side and bit me.

I was about to staunch the flow of blood with a hot poker and stitch the wound up with a bit of baling twine, but my wife insisted on putting a pressure pad on it and taking me to the local hospital!

Reporting my accident to my editor, I got a guffaw of sympathy as he announced my misfortune to the entire staff of GMC Publications. Fortunately the injury, though painful, was minor and healed well – served as a very effective reminder to concentrate, to always keep hands at least 4in (100mm) away from machine blades, and to use push sticks!

Screw fitting sides to foot post

FINISHING

Once the bed was complete and I was sure everything fitted properly, it was taken to pieces for finishing – giving me back a large proportion of my workshop's limited floor space! Most of the sanding had been completed during the construction, so the pieces were finally checked over, any marks and glue ooze removed, and the surfaces which would be visible hand sanded down to 240-grit prior to varnishing. I use Siafast hand sanding blocks, with a hard face for flat areas, and a soft face to follow profiles and curves, both with the Velcro system for attaching sheets. I have several blocks, with different grit grades fitted, to save time.

To keep the fresh, clean, natural look of the ash I chose a satin finish, water based, acrylic floor varnish. I applied three coats with a paint pad, rubbing down with 320-grit between coats, to denib. The advantage of the acrylic finishes on pale woods is that they have a minimal initial yellowing effect, and prevent long term darkening by filtering out UV light.

Barfords Aquacote is my preferred water-based varnish as it dries quickly, allowing you to apply up to five coats in a day and cures in a few days to a very tough, durable surface. I also use the new matt finish extensively as it has a much lower sheen than the satin and is just as tough and durable.

After the varnish had cured for a few days I cut it back with a Scotchbrite grey pad, applied a couple of coats of wax and buffed it up to a nice sheen. The wax on the ash gave a nice, touchy-feely surface – appropriate for bedroom furniture. The floor of the bedroom was bare wood, so I fitted self-adhesive felt pads to the underside of the leg posts to allow the bed to slide without making scuff marks.

HEIGHT OF PERFECTION

Once the bed was assembled in the room it looked great, suiting the cottage well and looking bright and fresh. I suppose in the final analysis all I had really achieved was an increase in sleeping altitude of 18in (460mm) or so but, most importantly, Yvonne was pleased. So much so that after a long pause, she said, 'Now – about that bedside chest of drawers...' Turn to page 100!

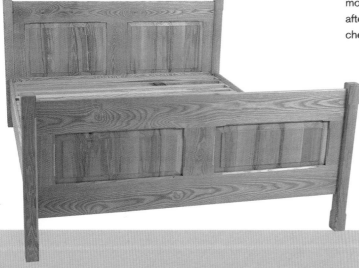

Bedside manners

Project 9 Project

This pair of bedside chests of drawers came next in my task of replacing the furniture which I had sold with our farmhouse (for details of the bed, see pages 95–99). I was pleased to be able to replace those pieces – I had made them early in my professional career and my taste and abilities had changed – for the better, I hope. Yvonne had also arrived on the scene and her trained artist's eye, and articulate opinions had become a welcome influence.

I was keen to furnish the new cottage with my own pieces in order to use it as a live-in showroom, as I had done very successfully with the farmhouse. Fortunately we both enjoy an eclectic mix of woods and styles which enables me to show a lot of options, in a relatively small space.

I also, initially, get great satisfaction from living with something I have made. Later, as the novelty wears off, it becomes a reminder of my limitations, when I realize how the piece could have been improved.

I can also test theories and new products – such as biscuit joints and modern adhesives – over the longer term, in real-life conditions. I must say that in a house full of my own furniture, with innumerable housing joints, not a single one shows any sign of self-destructing.

Kevin adds a brace of bedside chests of drawers to his newly made ash bed

The chests were made to complement the traditional vernacular-style bed

Shooting the carcass joints
for the tops, sides and base

Routing the housings
for the drawer divisions

Removing the
waste for dovetails

FOLLOWING THE THEME

The bed (see pages 95–99) had been a traditional design and we decided to continue this theme in the bedside pieces. The functional requirement was for a small drawer space, a resting place for early morning cups of coffee, and the odd late-night glass of malt whisky.

The key measurement was the height of the top, relative to the person on the mattress. Over the years I have found that, as a rule of thumb, the top of a bedside table should be about level with the top surface of the mattress.

Rather than having all the drawers the same depth, I decided to increase the size towards the base. This was not only visually more pleasing, but functionally more practical for the kit to be stored. The remaining features and measurements were decided upon and a sketch made on the white board in the workshop. I rarely work directly from paper drawings – instead, I generally transfer the sketch and cutting list to the white board, drawn large, for ease of working.

SPARE PARTS

Left over from the bed were a number of good-sized offcuts of English ash (*Fraxinus excelsior*), with a lot of olive and brown marbling effect. It had been a bit too fussy to use on the bed, where we had restricted the colour to the fielded panels, but would be ideal for these cabinets. The wood was thoroughly conditioned, having come from my dehumidified wood store, to the even warmer and drier workshop for the bed project. All the spare pieces had been sticked and stacked to keep them ready for use.

English ash is a very versatile timber, ranging in colour from very white – much in demand for sports equipment and striking tool handles – to a deep brown and grey heartwood, similar in appearance to Mediterranean olive, and called 'olive ash'. Ripple ash is rarer, similar to ripple sycamore, with the ripple grain running at right angles to the main grain. If you are very lucky the ripple and olive colour are combined to give a stunning effect. The individuality of

this timber can be a wonderful advantage – if it doesn't come as a surprise to your client.

Ash is readily available, at good prices, compared with more widely used woods such as oak. It is tough and durable, works easily, has an open, but even, straight grain, and can be brought to an excellent smooth finish.

CONSTRUCTION

TOPS, BASES AND SIDES

The pieces of timber for the carcass were faced and thicknessed to ⅞in (22mm) and laid out on the workshop floor. I selected the best figure for the top face of each of the tops, and continued this figure through the sides. I kept to the natural look, with the darker figure towards the middle, and paler wood towards the outside edges. The bases were given lowest priority as they had both faces hidden.

Once I had arranged the pieces I marked them, cut them to size, and edge-jointed them with biscuit reinforcing. I machined the edges straight, and hand-planed them to remove planer ripples, leaving the edge slightly concave to make sure there was pressure on the ends, thus allowing for extra shrinkage during drying.

The sides, tops, and bases were glued, clamped up, and cut to exact size when set. Stopped housings ⅞ x ¼in (22 x 6mm) were routed in the tops and bases to take the sides, and a ¼ x ¼in (6 x 6mm) slot was routed in the inside faces of the bases, tops, and sides to take the ¼in (6mm) ply backs. The sides were slotted for biscuits to take the drawer frames.

I rounded over the edges of the tops and bases with a ⅜in (10mm) radius cutter on the router table, and finished the edges of the sides with a plane. All were then belt- and orbital-sanded down to 120-grit, and sticked and stacked out of the way.

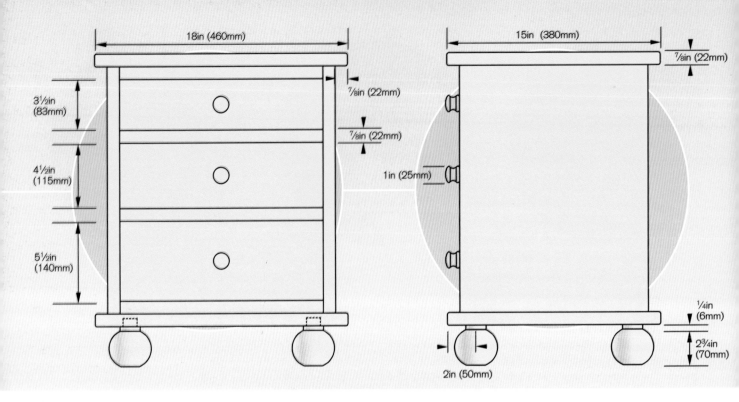

18in (460mm)

3½in (83mm)

4½in (115mm)

5½in (140mm)

⅞in (22mm)

⅞in (22mm)

15in (380mm)

⅞in (22mm)

1in (25mm)

¼in (6mm)

2¾in (70mm)

2in (50mm)

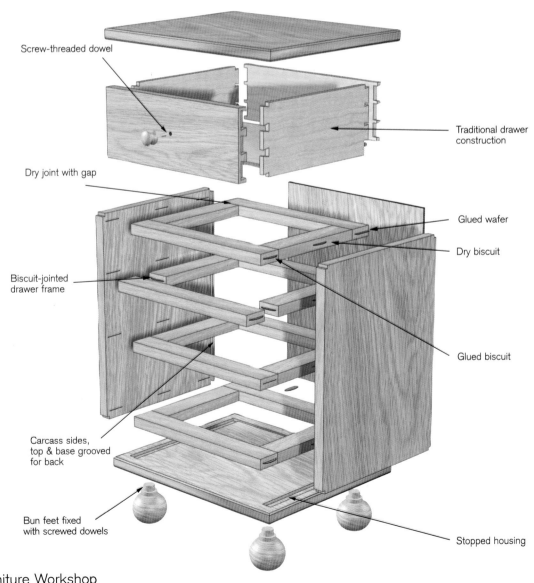

Screw-threaded dowel

Traditional drawer construction

Dry joint with gap

Glued wafer

Dry biscuit

Biscuit-jointed drawer frame

Glued biscuit

Carcass sides, top & base grooved for back

Bun feet fixed with screwed dowels

Stopped housing

Smooth operations

All the pieces had been power sanded down to 120-grit, first with a belt, then with an orbital sander during construction. All that was now required was to check them over for marks, glue ooze, and blemishes, which were removed with 120-grit on a Siafast hand sanding block.

I was using the same water-based, satin finish, acrylic varnish, as I had on the bed. I had noticed then that the grain of the ash was seriously raised by the first coat, making it necessary to rub it down again with 240-grit. I decided to apply the first coat at this stage rather than rub down twice with 240-grit.

I applied the varnish with a felt paint pad – by far the best method I have found as the paint pads are cheap, can be washed, and never seem to wear out! They are quick, give a nice even coat, leave no brush marks, and shed no bristles.

I applied the first coat, left it for three hours in the warm, dry workshop, and rubbed it down with 240-grit. I applied the second coat in the same way and rubbed it down with with 320-grit, and the third and last coat I left for three days, then cut it back with a Scotchbrite grey pad, waxed and buffed to a nice sheen.

DRAWERS AND BACKS

I made the drawer frames from 2in (50mm)-wide pieces of ⅞in (22mm) ash, biscuit-jointed at the corners – I used no. 20 size and trimmed the excess. Those at the front were glued up in the usual way, but those at the back were left dry and a gap provided between the side and back rail to allow for movement across the grain in the sides.

I cut biscuit slots in the frame sides, at the front and the centre, to fit the frames to the sides. The ends of the back rails were slotted with a 4mm router cutter to take Tanseli wafers, cut to size as loose tenons.

I cut the backs from some ash-faced ¼in ply I had lying around. I greatly favour sheet material for backs wherever possible, so I can glue the backs in all round and pin and glue them to the backs of rails and shelves to increase their strength – particularly against racking. Solid backs can't be fitted in this way as they will move.

The complete brace of cabinets

ASSEMBLING THE CARCASSES

I assembled each carcass in three stages – first I fitted the frames to the sides, then I glued the backs and pinned them into position, and finally I dropped the tops and bases on. It was summer and very warm and I felt that Titebond might 'grab' a bit too fast, so I decided to use PVA for its longer 'open' time.

All the joints on the sides and drawer frames were checked for fit while still dry, the clamps prepared, and set to size. The front biscuits were glued in the usual way, the centre biscuits left dry as locators, but allowing for movement across the grain of the sides. I glued the rear loose tenons to the rear rail ends and the sides, taking care not to bridge the movement gap between the rear rail and the side of the frame.

After clamping up, I measured the diagonals, front and back, to check for square, and left both the carcasses to set. Next I glued the backs into the slots in the sides and glued and pinned to the rear frame rails.

I applied PVA glue to the stopped housings in the tops and bases. They were located on to the sides and backs, then I tapped them home with my rubber mallet and clamped up. I re-measured diagonals to check all was still square and left the completed carcasses to set. When set, I drilled the holes for the dowels on the bun feet.

BUN FEET AND PULLS

While the carcasses were setting I went to the lathe to turn the bun feet and drawer pulls. This is about the limit of my turning skill, so I tend to rely on my sizing tools to get things at least the same diameters – any slight discrepancies in the shapes are rarely noticed if things are not too close together!

I had kept the offcuts from the 3in (75mm)-thick ash from which the bed posts had been cut, and was able to get enough 3 x 3 x 3in (75 x 75 x 75mm) blanks for the feet, and some 1¼ x 1¼ x 1¼in (31 x 31 x 31mm) blanks for the pulls. These were all turned, leaving a dowel on the end for fitting, and sanded to a finish.

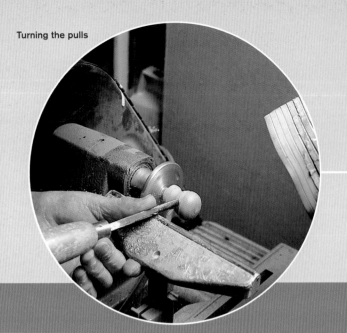

'I was using the same water-based, satin finish, acrylic varnish, as I had on the bed. I had noticed then that the grain of the ash was seriously raised by the first coat'

Bed and bedside chests of drawers in situ

MAKING THE DRAWERS

The drawer fronts and casings were cut to size, fitted and marked. The fronts were made from ⅞in (22mm) ash, allowing some individuality in the figure. The rest of the casings were from ⅜in (10mm) cedar of Lebanon (*Cedrela spp*) for its wonderful scent, which repels moths, but seems to attract clients! The bases were MDF-faced with cedar of Lebanon, which is expensive, but I think worth it.

The fronts were drilled to receive the dowels on the end of the pulls. The sides were slotted for the bases, taped together in double pairs, with the top one marked out, the tails cut out on the bandsaw, and finished with a paring chisel.

I marked the pins on the drawer fronts and backs with a scalpel, one at a time, from the corresponding tails, and removed most of the waste with a router. I then finished each joint individually with a sharp paring chisel, sanded the insides to a finish and assembled the drawer. I glued the MDF base in all round, and glued and screwed it at the back, checked it for square and wind and left it to set.

I fitted the drawers into their positions in the carcasses, and marked the back face of the back to identify which cabinet they belonged to. I fitted stops to the front rails and sanded the outsides of the drawers to a finish. The pulls were not fitted at this point.

FIT AND FINISH

The pulls and feet were much easier to finish before fitting, as were the drawer fronts without the pulls fitted, and the carcasses without the feet. When the finish had cured, double-ended, screw-threaded dowels, were fitted to the pulls, glue applied to the dowel on the end and the pulls screwed into place in the drawer fronts. The bun feet were fitted in a similar way to the pre-drilled holes in the underside of the base, and self-adhesive felt buttons fixed to the underside of the feet.

SATISFYING CONCLUSION

These chests were not difficult and did not take long to make, but at last we had somewhere for the bedside lights, clock radio, books, drinks, etc. We also had an extra six drawers-worth of storage space, and I had gained some serious Brownie points!

The Arts &

Crafts set 1

The bedroom in our new cottage needed some serious hanging and drawer space. This wardrobe and chest of drawers unit completes the bedroom set – see pages 95–99 for the bed, and pages 100–104 for the bedside chests of drawers.

Built-in wardrobes, and relatively cheap flat-pack units have made wardrobes a fairly rare and comparatively expensive bespoke item, but we decided to indulge ourselves, secure in the knowledge that in any future move we would be able to take our clothes storage space with us. That is, of course, if I don't sell it all again with the house!

Kevin completes his Arts and Crafts-style bedroom suite by making a mighty fine wardrobe in American white ash

'KISS' (Keep It Simple Soldier) is the key to knock-down furniture

⬤ DESIGN TIME

The bedroom is a large, airy, room with a pine floor and no clutter. Even with the king-sized bed, the bedside chests, a Shaker-style dressing-table and chair, and an Arts and Crafts-style tall chest in sycamore and fumed oak, there was still plenty of room for a large free-standing piece.

We had briefly considered a built-in unit, with solid doors or a curtain front. A curtain front can soften a large unit, provide a link with other soft furnishings in the room and requires less floor space as no clearance is needed for the doors to open.

We also thought about a Shaker-style floor-to-ceiling fitted storage unit with various arrangements of drawers, shelves and hanging space. The Shakers did this a lot – their obsession with cleanliness and the efficiency of attaining it, made them regard high, inaccessible tops as dust traps.

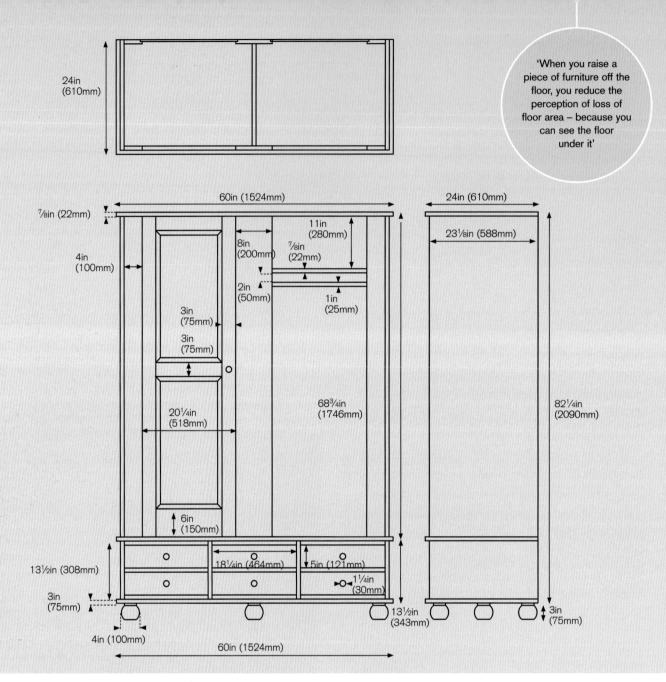

'When you raise a piece of furniture off the floor, you reduce the perception of loss of floor area – because you can see the floor under it'

In the end we decided that any built-in storage reduced the flexibility of the room layout and would not achieve the look we wanted, so we went for a free-standing unit, combining drawer and hanging space. The drawer space should be at low level, with the hanging space above. High-level drawers always seem to be a bit of a nonsense to me – you have to lift them right out and bring them down to see inside!

● A GAME OF TWO HALVES

With a piece this size, its weight, handling and the access to the room are major considerations. It quickly became evident that the wardrobe would not be manageable as a single piece. It was easy to split it into two – the base six-drawer unit and the top cupboard. Even so the top cupboard was still too big to get into the room in one piece. Thus was born my first piece of 'flat-pack' furniture.

The top cupboard would be made as finished components – top, base, sides, partition, shelves, rails, backs, and doors. The carcass would be screwed together, so that it could be assembled and disassembled in the workshop, then finished and reassembled in the bedroom. I do enjoy a challenge!

I would have to take great care to ensure rigidity – particularly as it would have inset doors. Any 'diamonding' or 'ricking' of the carcass would cause door problems. I decided to continue the sides around with a fixed front and back return, making a 'U' cross-section, and the same with the central partition, giving it an 'I' cross-section. The top and base would be screwed on, and sheet material backs screwed into rebates.

The base drawer unit was modelled on a 'stretched' version of the bedside chests, using six drawers so that the join between the two cupboards above was bridged, and it did not look like two cupboards stuck together. I kept the

Selecting the timber

I had made the bed and chests from English ash (*Fraxinus excelsior*) using some of the colour in the through and through boards, to add interest. As this was such a big piece we decided that white ash, without the olive colour, would be less fussy.

Remembering how pleased I had been with the American maple (*Acer spp*) used in the Morris seating, I decided to look at some American white ash (*Fraxinus spp*) at my local Timberworld. It turned out to be very similar in looks and properties to English white ash, and came in long, clean, wide, straight- edged boards, at a price similar to soft-woods. It was a lot cheaper than buying 'through and through' English ash boards and the colour was more consistent, which suited me for this project.

I find it difficult to understand how American timber can have all the waste removed, be cut into straight-edged planks, brought several thousand miles, and delivered to my door, cheaper than wood growing and processed a few miles away. I took a piece home, found it to blend well with the existing bedroom pieces, and made up an order. The straight-edged boards, long lengths and availability of vari-ous widths of plank made it easy to minimize wastage.

The internal shelves, partition, and drawer casings were from cedar of Lebanon (*Cedrela odorata*) for its scent and moth-repellent quality. For the sake of consistency, the backs and drawer bases were made from MDF, faced with cedar of Lebanon. This was an expensive decision, as the backs and bases are hardly seen, in use, and that piece of MDF cost ten times more than a similar piece of plain MDF or plywood.

Timber preparation

Although the ash had been kiln-dried at source there was no way of knowing what had happened to it since, so I treated it to an extended time, stacked and sticked, in my timber store, with the dehumidifier working hard! The cedar came from stock which had already been there for some time, so it was ready for use.

Once the workshop had been cleared the timber was moved in, a cutting list produced, and the larger pieces cut first, selecting those with the best figure for the front. The progressively smaller pieces came from the remainder. All the pieces were cut slightly oversize and stacked, with sticks between, in the workshop where they continued to condition.

The cutting out, as usual, took much time and consideration. What was done at this stage would decide the final look, and as this is a particularly large piece, it would be a major feature in the room.

Next I faced, thicknessed, and re-stacked all the pieces for the entire project. Given that I am very careful to keep timber flat and sticked to allow even drying to all surfaces, all this handling in my warm dry workshop, aided the settling and drying of the timber before the making began.

Base chest carcass with drawer frames fitted

bun feet, and added an extra one, out of sight, in the centre of the base, for even weight distribution. Lifting this large piece off the floor would also lighten its look.

When you raise a piece of furniture off the floor, you reduce the perception of loss of floor area – because you can see the floor under it. In modern fitted kitchens floor units are sometimes put on quite tall legs, even with lights underneath the cabinet bases at floor level to accentuate the effect.

clearance depth of at least 20in (510mm), and full-length hanging height of about 5ft (1525mm). An option is to have some of the space as half-height hanging for shirts, jackets and the like, and use the space under for shelves or drawers. We decided that the overall size of the individual cupboards and the returns made this impractical.

⬤ CLEAR DIVISION

I kept the design of the upper cupboards very simple, with a high shelf for storage and a hanging rail. The fixed central partition was essential to clearly define which space belonged to whom! I am always amazed at the ability of Yvonne's clothes to migrate into any spare space in my tidy wardrobe, and live in mortal fear of inadvertently incorporating the wrong item in my outfit and being drummed out of GMC Publications! In order to hang clothes sideways on to the door, a wardrobe needs an internal

⬤ DESIGN FOOTNOTE

I gave some extra height for shoe storage under the hanging clothes. The overall look of the piece was kept as clean and simple as possible, with a rounded overhanging top and base and bun feet to match the bedside chests. For the doors I chose a simple frame and fielded panel, with a centre rail, internal hanging rails for ties, belts, and scarves, and piano hinges for strength and a clean line.

CONSTRUCTION

First I made all the flat components. This method of construction made the most of the limited space in my workshop, as I could stick and stack all the pieces in one pile, and allow the timber to continue to condition for as long as possible, before final making-up. Once I'd completed the 'flats' I made the drawer unit, then the top cupboard.

⬤ MAKING THE FLATS

These consisted of:

- The top of the top cupboard
- The base of the top cupboard, which was also the top of the drawer unit
- The base of the drawer unit
- Sides and partition of the top cupboard without the fronts or backs attached
- The shelves of the top unit
- The sides and partitions of the drawer unit

I made all the flats in the same way, from the thicknessed pieces already cut slightly over-width and length. I machine-planed the edges straight, then hand-planed them to remove the planer ripples and leave the joint slightly hollow in the centre, allowing for extra shrinkage at the ends.

This shrinkage is caused by the end grain losing moisture quicker than the rest for a short distance into the plank.

I reinforced the joints with biscuits at about 12in (305mm) centres, and glued and clamped them up. Once the joints were dry, I scraped the glue lines to remove glue ooze, and belt-sanded the faces down to 120-grit.

When dealing with this sort of area of wood, the belt sander really comes into its own – imagine doing all this acreage of wood with a smoothing plane, scraper, and sanding block!

Next I cut the pieces to size exactly, keeping a check on the diagonal measurements to ensure they were square.

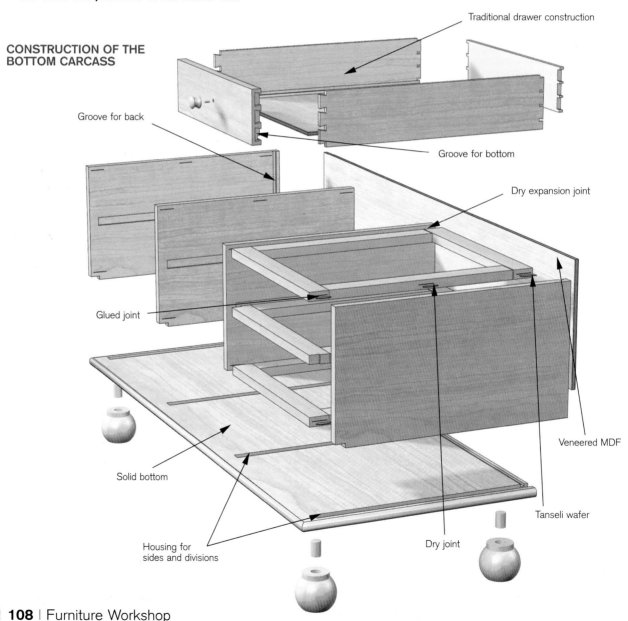

CONSTRUCTION OF THE BOTTOM CARCASS

Traditional drawer construction

Groove for back

Groove for bottom

Dry expansion joint

Glued joint

Veneered MDF

Solid bottom

Tanseli wafer

Housing for sides and divisions

Dry joint

Screws and biscuits are used to fix and locate the top to the base carcass

The base carcass is now complete

MAKING THE BASE UNIT

To make the six-drawer base unit, I began by routing stopped housings ⅞ x ¼in (22 x 6mm) in the inside faces of the sides and both faces of the partitions of the base unit, to take the centre drawer rails. I routed a ¼ x ¼in (6 x 6mm) slot in the inside faces of the sides and base to take the 6mm-MDF back. I slotted the sides and partitions for biscuits to take the top and bottom drawer frames.

I rounded over the edges of the base with a ⅜in-radius cutter on the router table, and finished the edges of the sides and partitions with a plane. All were then belt- and orbital-sanded, down to 120-grit, and sticked and stacked, out of the way.

DRAWER FRAMES

To make up the drawer frames I used 2in (50mm)-wide pieces of ⅞in (22mm) ash, jointed at the corners with no. 20 size biscuits with any excess trimmed. I glued up those at the front in the usual way but left those at the back dry, and provided a gap between the side and back rail, to allow for movement across the grain in the sides.

I cut biscuit slots in the frame sides, at the front and the centre, to fit the frames to the sides. Then I slotted the ends of the back rails with a 4mm router cutter to take Tanseli wafers cut to size as loose tenons.

CUTTING THE BACK

I cut the back from 6mm MDF, which would be be glued in all round, and pinned and glued to the backs of rails to give strength against racking. I ensured that the top of the back finished flush with the top face of the top rail, and did not project into the base of the top cupboard unit.

CARCASS ASSEMBLY

Before the carcass was assembled all the pieces were further sanded down to 150-grit with an orbital sander, so that after assembly only the outside faces would require final finishing by hand.

The sequence was to fit the frames to the sides and partitions, then glue and pin the back into position, and finally drop the carcass on to the base.

As it would take some time to set up the frames, sides, and partitions for the initial clamp-up I check-fitted all the joints dry, prepared the clamps, and set them to size. Titebond might have grabbed too fast, so I used PVA for its longer open time.

On the top and bottom rails I glued the front biscuits in the usual way, leaving the centre biscuits dry as locators and weight bearers, but allowing for movement across the grain of the sides. The rear loose tenons were glued to the rear rail ends and the sides, taking care not to bridge the movement gap between the rear rail and the side rail of the frame.

The centre rails were set into stopped housings and glue was only applied to the front and back rail ends, again taking care not to bridge the movement gap, with the frame side rails running dry in the stopped housings.

After clamping up, I measured the diagonals, front and back, to check for square and left the carcass to set. Next I glued the back into the slots in the sides and glued and pinned it to the rear frame rails and partition back edges. The bottom edge of the back projected ¼in (6mm) proud of the bottom face of the bottom rail, and would fit into the slot in the base in due course.

Next I applied PVA glue to the stopped housings in the base, and located the carcass onto it, tapped it home and clamped it up. I measured diagonals again to check all was still square and left the completed carcass to set.

The Arts &

Crafts set 2

In the previous section, I designed the wardrobe, selected and cut the timber, and made the flat pieces, drawer frames and base carcass. Now I will explain how to complete the wardrobe.

Kevin completes his Arts and Crafts-style wardrobe in American white ash

BUN FEET AND PULLS

Once the glue has set on the base, drill the holes for the bun-feet dowels. To make the 4 x 4 x 3in (100 x 100 x 75mm) blanks for the bun feet I glue up matching pieces of 2 x 2in (50 x 50mm) English ash (Fraxinus excelsior) from stock, from which I also get the 1¼ x 1¼ x 1½in (32 x 32 x 38mm) blanks for the pulls. Turn the bun feet, door and drawer pulls at the same time, using sizing tools to get all the diameters the same – this will help mask any slight discrepancies in the shapes. A ½in (12mm) dowel is turned on the end of the pulls, and a 1in (25mm) dowel on the bun feet, for fitting – all sanded to a finish on the lathe.

THE TOP CUPBOARD

Make the stopped housings for the shelves with a router, and drill the blind holes for the hanging rails in the sides and partition. Cut rebates in the top, base and back returns of the sides and partition, to take the cedar of Lebanon-faced MDF backs. Finish all the returns, sides and the partition with an orbital sander to 120-grit.

Next, butt-joint the front and back returns with biscuit reinforcement, to the sides and partition, ensuring that they are at right-angles, before clamping up. The side components should now have the 'U' cross-section and the partition the 'I' cross-section, for stability.

Cut the cedar of Lebanon shelves to size and round over the front edges, then finish them to thickness and shoulder them to fit in the prepared stopped housings in the sides and partition. The hanging rails are cut to length from some 1in (25mm) bright steel tubing. Round over the front and side edges of the top and base with a ⅜in radius cutter and finish both to 120-grit with an orbital sander.

Wardrobes are very functional, but this makes them, of necessity, a big bit of furniture. Knock-down construction is the answer

The finished wardrobe
with both doors open

The inside faces of the doors
have rails for ties, belts and scarves

Cleaning up the doors

Final assembly: driving home
the screws, holding it all firm
with cramps

Cut biscuit slots in the ends of the side assemblies and the central partition assembly, and cut matching slots in the top and base. Cut the location biscuit slots in the underside of the top base and the top edges of the base unit to fit the base of the top unit to the top of the base drawer unit. Check-fit the common base/top to the drawer unit and make adjustments as necessary.

Assemble the top cupboard on its back, using dry biscuits in the slots as locators. Also fit the shelves and hanging rails dry. Make adjustments to ensure everything is in the correct position and square, and apply sash clamps.

I drilled counter-sunk pilot holes for the screws through the top and base and then fitted them. I removed the clamps and stood the partially assembled top unit carcass upright. I cut the cedar of Lebanon-faced MDF backs to size and measured the diagonals of the carcass to ensure it was square and screwed the backs into position.

⬤ MAKING THE DOORS

Measure the front openings, cut the doors, stiles and rails to size and make double biscuit joints between them. Dry-assemble the doors and take measurements for the fielded panels, recessing them ¼in (6mm) into the frame.

Make the door panels up by deep sawing some selected ash and match jointing. Use biscuits, positioned so that they will not be exposed by the fielding, to strengthen the joint.

Cut the panels to size and field them using a vertical profile cutter, then use a hand shoulder plane and sand them to finish. Finish the panel faces, cut a slot on the inside edges of the rails and stiles to take them, and finish the inside edges of the frames. Assemble, glue and clamp the doors, check for square and wind, and leave to set.

Making the drawers

I made the drawers in the same way as the drawers for the bedside chests (see pages 100–104). I made the fronts from ⅞in (22mm) ash, the remainder of the casings from ⅜in (10mm) cedar of Lebanon (*Cedrela ororata*) for its fragrance and insect repelling qualities and the drawer bases from cedar of Lebanon-faced MDF to match.

Cut the fronts, sides and backs to size, fit and mark them. Cut a slot in each side for the base, and tape them together in double pairs, with the tails marked on the top side. I cut most of the waste on the bandsaw to form the tails, which were finished exactly with a paring chisel.

Mark the pins on the drawer fronts and backs with a scalpel, one at a time, from the corresponding tails, and remove most of the waste with a router. Finish each joint individually with a sharp paring chisel.

Sand the insides of the drawers to a finish, drill the fronts for the pull dowels, and assemble each drawer. Glue the MDF base in all round, and glue and screw it to the back. Check the assembled drawer for square and wind, and leave to set.

Fit the drawers into their positions in the carcass, and mark them on the back face of the back for identification. Fit stops to the front rails, and sand the outsides of the drawers to a finish. The pulls and bun feet are not fitted at this point.

● FITTING THE DOORS

Once they are set, sand the faces of the door frames and fit the completed doors to the opening, leaving about ½in (1mm) clearance all round, to be adjusted to ⅝in (2mm) on final fitting. Use full-length piano hinges on these doors, as they give extra strength, leave a neat line, and even out the load. The hinges do not need to be recessed and a self-centring hinge pilot drill and a power screwdriver, make short work of fitting them.

Mark the position of the hinges on the inside face of the cupboard, and use a cutting gauge to scribe the screw line. One way to hold the doors at the correct height is by wedging a metal rule as a spacer underneath them.

Centre the screw line in the hinge screw hole and use the self-centring pilot drill to drill a pilot hole at the top, middle, and bottom of each hinge. Drive the screws home and check the door for fit. Make adjustments, screw the remaining holes and drive in the screws. Fit brass double ball-catches top and bottom, and adjust the springs to get a satisfying 'clunk-click'.

● ACCESSORY RAILS

Make rails for the inside face of the doors – ideal for hanging ties, scarves and belts. My original intention was to have a high and low rail on each door for use by the owner of that half of the wardrobe, but in fact I had to have both the high rails as I hadn't realised how high the top rail would be – and Yvonne can't reach!

● FINISHING

For ease and convenience of finishing, I disassembled the top unit. I had done all the power-sanding on the individual components before assembly. Now I could do the final sanding by palm sander and hand blocks. As with the other items in this room I used a water-based satin varnish, to keep the pale colour of the ash (*Fraxinus spp.*). It is an acrylic floor varnish that dries quickly and hardens to a tough finish.

To do the same, apply the first coat with a paint pad before sanding it by hand, as the grain is raised considerably by the water base. Sand down this coat with 240-grit on a Siafast block, then apply a further coat with the paint pad and rub down with 320-grit on the same block. Leave a third coat for seven days in the warm, dry workshop to fully cure and then cut it back with a Scotchbrite grey pad.

The inside faces, which included all the cedar of Lebanon were not varnished – I only sealed them with wax, in order to allow the scent to permeate freely. I was careful to use masking tape to protect the bare edges when I applied the varnish.

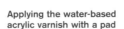

Applying the water-based
acrylic varnish with a pad

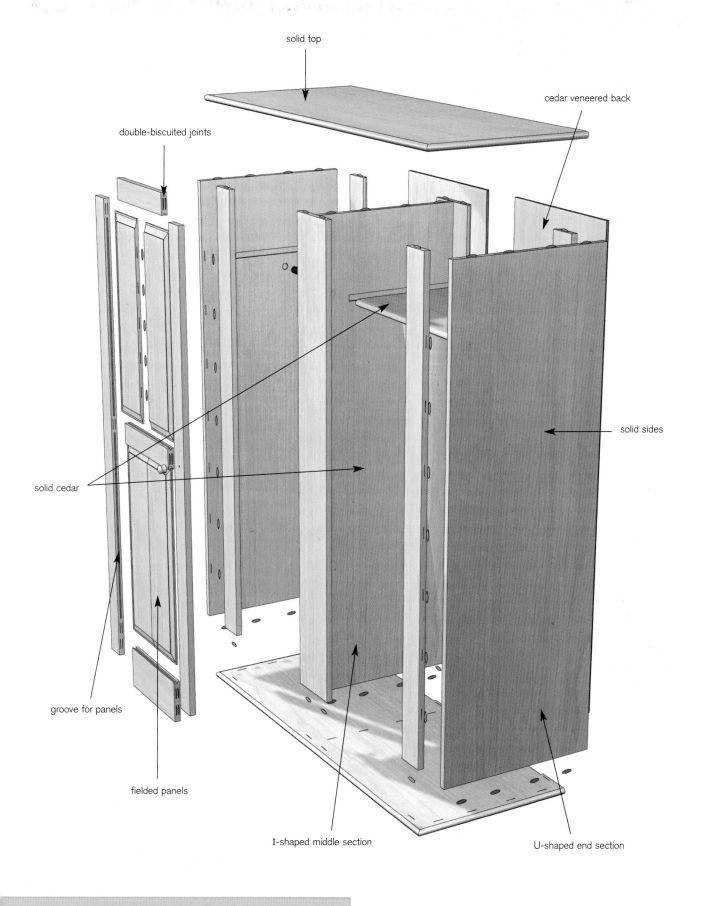

solid top

cedar veneered back

double-biscuited joints

solid sides

solid cedar

groove for panels

fielded panels

I-shaped middle section

U-shaped end section

'I enjoyed the challenge of this piece –
it certainly meets our requirements and
looks great in position'

Close-up of bun foot
and base overhang

After assembly, pads
were added to the feet

FEET AND PULLS

I finished the feet and pulls at the same time and glued and screwed them into position.

ASSEMBLY IN SITU

Yvonne and I carried the drawer unit base up to the destination room without too much trouble, though it was not light. Then we took the component parts of the top cupboard up and placed them carefully around the room.

We laid a large blanket over the pine floor and assembled the top cupboard on it, on its back. When we stood it upright it presented quite a problem to get it onto the drawer base. I had not needed to do this in the workshop, once I'd check-fitted the common base/top, but now the full weight and awkwardness was apparent.

In the end I lifted one end while Yvonne slid the drawer unit under, then I lifted the other end and slid it onto the base. It was heavy and really needed two strong lifters. There was the danger of it tipping or sliding off but all went well and we managed to get it into position.

I rocked the top to lift the front and back and each side separately, allowing Yvonne to drop the locating biscuits into place. Once it was in position I drove home the screws to attach it to the base. Then the whole unit was not difficult to slide into position because the felt buttons under the bun feet slid easily on the smooth wooden floor.

I checked that all the bun feet were bearing weight and applied small chocks where necessary to level it all up. The doors were hung and all tests and adjustments made, then two coats of wax were applied to the outside and finally buffed up to a nice sheen.

OVERVIEW

I enjoyed the challenge of this piece – it certainly meets our requirements and looks great in position. Its pale colour prevents it from dominating the room and also acts as a reflector, throwing light in. Rigidity has been good and there have been no door problems. Its own weight – around 300lbs, contributes to its stability.

For some time after it went in, I regularly checked the ceiling in the room below for bowing, and that the back remained parallel with the wall it was against. To date no sag has become apparent so the oak ceiling beams downstairs can obviously cope!

An interesting case

Kevin combines Brazilian mahogany and English cherry to make a classic bookcase

I had made a large partners' desk for a client and when I installed it at his town house, we discussed the storage arrangements in the room. It was apparent that he needed more shelf storage for books, CDs, videos and files, something easily accessible and convenient to the desk. We agreed that a floor-to-ceiling bookcase was required.

DESIGN

My client's home is a 19th-century town house constructed of traditional, solid stone, with good sized, well-proportioned rooms and high ceilings.

The bookcase was to fit in a recess on one side of a chimney breast next to the desk in the study, which is well lit with a tall French window opening onto the garden. A simple honest design in solid wood seemed to be the most suitable option, blending in well with the surroundings.

My client was a big fan of the fumed mahogany (*Swietenia macrophylla*) and English cherry (*Prunus avium*) used for the desk and wanted a bookcase that matched. We decided on glazed doors to reduce dusting, with the door frames in cherry and the rest of the piece in fumed mahogany. As the bookcase is in a recess, only the front is really in full view so the cherry has a good impact.

TIMBER SELECTION

I ordered the best-quality Brazilian mahogany (*Swietenia macrophylla*) available from my local joinery supplier. He had a good quality range in different sizes, enabling me to buy with little waste, and I'm pleased to say that the timber was certified from a sustainable, legal source. Fortunately my local area has quite a lot of wild English cherry and I was able to get some good quality stock from a timberyard close by.

The base unit

The top unit

TIMBER PREPARATION

Mark out and cut the components oversize, stick them and leave for some weeks to settle in a timber store. A dehumidifier is a real bonus here as it helps dry the wood. Final conditioning should take place during making in the workshop, which should also be kept at optimum conditions with a dehumidifier and sawdust burner. To avoid movement in service, the relative humidity levels in the workshop and timber store should be kept as close as possible to the conditions the piece will finally be housed in. Occasional makers can stack the timber on sticks in a spare bedroom, or even under a bed, for a few weeks. It should not be left all week in a cold damp garage either – bring it inside!

CONSTRUCTION

I decided against making adjustable shelves, as the structure is weakened and the shelves are rarely moved after the initial loading. A better method is to line up all the kit which is to go in it, and work out the shelf spacings required beforehand, allowing much stronger, permanent, shelf fixing. The client agreed with my recommendations and so I got to work.

Bearing in mind the weight of the books and the height of the piece, I wanted to add the 'lean back' feature frequently incorporated in tall, Victorian bookcases. The plinths were cut lower at the back so the bookcase leaned back with its weight against the wall behind it.

I decided not to build the lean into the cabinet but to use chocks when I installed it. This would also allow for the floor and walls in the house, which weren't exactly true and level, and the carpet-gripper edging strip against the skirting, which would lift the back and push the top forward away from the wall.

For flexibility of use, movement, and construction, we decided that the bookcase should be in two pieces – a shallower top cupboard sitting on a deeper base, located at the back with a metal bracket.

I produced drawings after taking all the relevant measurements, agreed the costings, and ordered the timber.

CARCASS CONSTRUCTION

All the components should now be thicknessed and cut to size, carefully checking for accuracy before making repeat cuts! Organize your work space so the components can be sticked and stacked flat during making, with free air flow to all faces for even drying. The backs from 6mm, mahogany-faced MDF should also be cut to size.

HOUSINGS

Using a router, cut stopped housings for the sides and partitions in the shelves – ⅞in (22mm) wide x ⁵⁄₁₆in (8mm) deep. Make similar stopped housings in the tops to take the sides and the partitions. Do the same in the bases of the top and bottom units. It's a good idea to cut housings in the sides of the bottom unit to take the base. Fit the base of the top unit with biscuits. Cut a ¼ x ¼in (6 x 6mm) in the sides and tops to take the backs.

Housing joints should be a compression fit, and require knocking home with a hammer and block. About 1mm of the leading edge of the male piece can be very slightly bevelled to assist in starting the entry. The glue should be spread quite thinly with a brush along the top edges of the housing, and thinly on the leading edges of the entering piece. It initially provides lubrication, then swells the wood to give a mechanical fit like a biscuit, and finally gives some, if limited, glue bond. It is a mechanical joint – a sloppy fit relying on glue as a filler is ineffective.

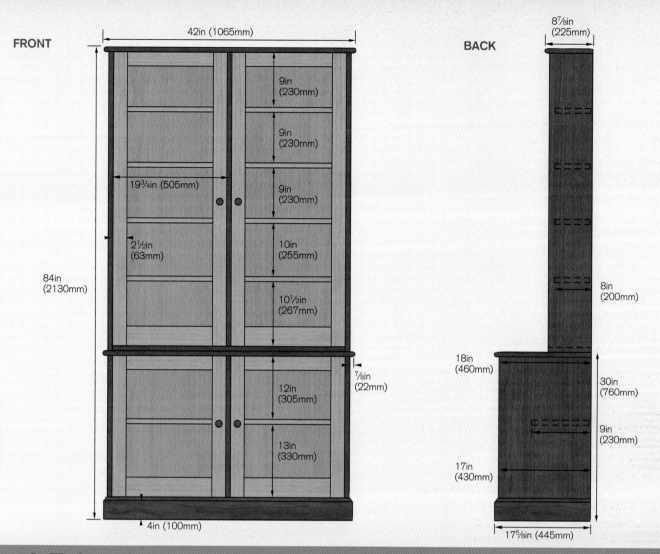

FRONT

42in (1065mm)

9in (230mm)

9in (230mm)

19¾in (505mm)

9in (230mm)

2½in (63mm)

10in (255mm)

10½in (267mm)

84in (2130mm)

⅞in (22mm)

12in (305mm)

13in (330mm)

4in (100mm)

BACK

8⅞in (225mm)

8in (200mm)

18in (460mm)

30in (760mm)

9in (230mm)

17in (430mm)

17⅝in (445mm)

A Tale of two timbers

BRAZILIAN MAHOGANY

Brazilian mahogany (*Swietenia macrophylla*) is the best replacement timber available for the legendary Cuban or Spanish mahogany used in period furniture for more than 200 years. It is no longer commercially available due to its indiscriminate exploitation.

This timber normally comes in straight-edged boards with little of the pale sapwood. The heartwood when first planed in the workshop can look pale pink but its light brown to deep browny-red characteristic colour is quickly brought out by age, exposure to light and air, fuming and the application of finishes, such as oil. It is moderately easy to work, having a fairly straight grain, though occasional interlocked pockets, which tend to tear, require a careful approach with a sharp, finely set, plane or scraper. It finishes to a medium texture and there is not much movement in use if it has been properly seasoned and conditioned.

ENGLISH CHERRY

This is a lovely straight-grained, finely textured, pale-brown timber which, like elm (*Ulmus spp*), sometimes has a green streak along the grain. The brown of the heartwood has a pink tinge which was an ideal colour link to the red of the fumed mahogany. It works well and finishes to a fine, silky surface although it can chip badly on the cross-grained patches.

Unfortunately it tends not to season well, being subject to splitting and warping, causing high wastage. This naturally increases its price and makes it wise to view the timber before you make the purchase. American cherry (*Prunus serotina*) is a completely different timber which is darker, redder, and cheaper!

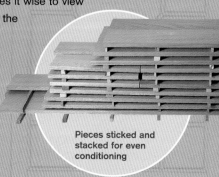

Pieces sticked and stacked for even conditioning

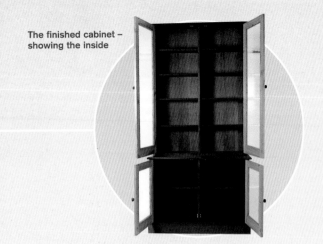

The finished cabinet – showing the inside

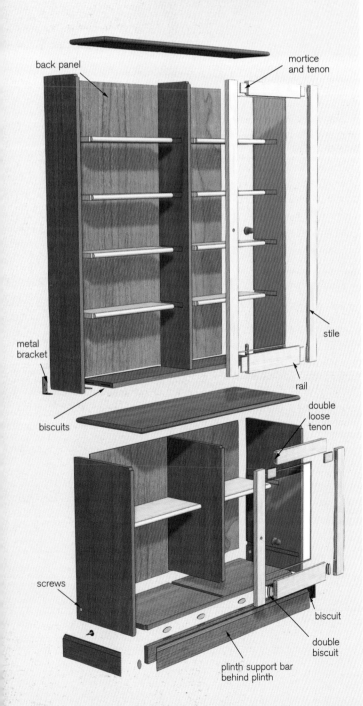

back panel

mortice and tenon

stile

metal bracket

rail

biscuits

double loose tenon

screws

biscuit

double biscuit

plinth support bar behind plinth

The joint is least strong in the direction from which it was assembled but has strength in all other areas. The housings in the tops, which are at right angles, together with the glued and screwed back, and the strengthening screws behind the plinth, provide strength against any outward spreading forces.

The sides, partitions, shelves, and base of the bottom unit were all shouldered, then the front edges of the shelves, and the front and side edges of the tops, were rounded over to ⅜in (10mm) radius.

ASSEMBLY

Give the piece the once-over with belt and orbital sanders and finish down to 150-grit. Dry-assemble each carcass to check that they fit. To make clamping easier, screw partitions through from under the bases to pull the housing tight. Countersink the screws and plug the holes.

The only difference in the assembly of the top and bottom units is that the base of the top is biscuited to the sides, while the base of the bottom is housed, just like the shelves.

With a brush, apply glue into the housings, fit the partition to the base, and screw into position. Then fit the base to the sides, and fit the shelves into the housings in the sides and partitions. Apply clamps, measure diagonals to check that all is square, and leave the unit to set.

Clamp the tops into position on the sides, check the carcass units for square, and leave to set.

BACKS

Apply glue to the back edges of the shelves, partition, base, and slots in the sides and tops. Then, place the pre-sanded back carefully in position and screw through to the shelves, partition, and base.

PLINTHS

Fit a support bar for the plinth front between the sides of the base unit. It should be screwed through the sides and biscuited to the base above it.

Apply an ogee moulding to the top edges of the plinth pieces with a router, cut to length, mitre on the radial arm saw, and finish on a shooting board.

Use biscuits in the mitres, which are very useful in preventing them slipping when clamped up. They also provide extra strength.

Fit the plinth front by screwing and gluing, from the back on to the support bar. The first 3in (75mm) of the plinth sides should also be glued and screwed to the sides, and clamped into position. Leave the remainder of the plinth sides dry. They should be fixed at the back, from the inside, through an oversize hole, with a screw and washer. This allows for movement across the grain of the sides. Once the mitres are dry, sand to a finish.

Edge planing the doors

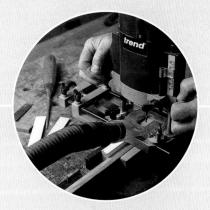

Cutting slots for loose tenons on the bottom doors with a spiral cutter

The bottom door frame showing the double biscuit on the bottom rail, and the double Tanseli wafer loose tenon on the top rail

DOORS

Cut the cherry door-frame pieces to size. While halfway through cutting the rails, I belatedly realized that I had not allowed for the tenons. Fortunately, I made an adjustment in time to enable the top door frames to be morticed and tenoned in the usual way.

I wasn't able to get a satisfactory match of good-quality cherry for new rails for the bottom doors, so as the bottom doors are quite small and not subject to excessive strain, I decided to use the short-cut ones. Double loose tenons from Tanseli wafers were used on the top joints which were too narrow for double no. 20 biscuits. The bottom rails were deeper and double biscuits were used on the bottom joints.

I have experimented with both these joints extensively, testing them to destruction in the workshop and using them on my own furniture. They have been entirely satisfactory as the wood has always broken before the joint, making little practical difference between them and mortice and tenon joints, in many applications.

Clamp up all the doors, check for square, and leave to set. For the glass and glazing bead, cut the rebates with a router on the inside of the frame. Carefully fit the unglazed door frames with brass butt-hinges and ball catches, then remove, power and hand-sand, and finish with three coats of acrylic varnish. This helps maintain the pale colour of the cherry.

Fit the glass into the frame with a ¹⁄₁₆in (1.5mm) clearance all round, on a very thin bed of clear silicone mastic. Pin the glazing bead carefully into position. The mahogany door pulls to be fumed with the carcass, can be turned on the lathe.

FUMING

Remove all the glue ooze and other dirty marks from the carcass, and hand-sand to a 320-grit finish. The next step is to make a tent frame over the carcass pieces, and cover it in thin polythene sheet. Place plastic tubs of ammonia 890 in the tent and weigh down the edges of the sheet to the floor with strips of wood to make it air tight. Concentrated ammonia is toxic, corrosive, and can cause permanent damage to the eyes on contact. As a precaution, always wear gloves and some form of eye protection.

FINISH

After fuming, finish the carcass with Danish oil to really bring out the deep colour of the mahogany. Apply a liberal first coat and renew it every hour or so for a day, until the timber can really take no more. I removed all the surplus, and left it to cure in a warm, dry workshop for 24 hours.

Cut back the surface by hand with 320-grit, followed by a light coat of oil every 24 hours for a week. Cut back between coats with a Scotchbrite grey pad and leave it for a couple of weeks to fully cure. Your piece should now be ready for delivery.

IMPERIAL/METRIC CONVERSION TABLE
inches to millimetres

in	mm	in	mm	in	mm	in	mm
1/64	0.3969	5/8	15.8750	2 3/4	69.8501	33	838.202
1/32	0.7937			2 7/8	73.0251	34	863.602
3/64	1.1906	41/64	16.2719	3	76.2002	35	889.002
1/16	1.5875	21/32	16.6687			36 (3ft)	914.402
5/64	1.9844	43/64	17.0656	3 1/8	79.3752		
3/32	2.3812	11/16	17.4625	3 1/4	82.5502	37	939.802
7/64	2.7781	45/64	17.8594	3 3/8	85.7252	38	965.202
1/8	3.1750	23/32	18.2562	3 1/2	88.9002	39	990.602
		47/64	18.6531	3 5/8	92.0752	40	1016.00
9/64	3.5719	3/4	19.0500	3 3/4	95.2502	41	1041.40
5/32	3.9687			3 7/8	98.4252	42	1066.80
11/64	4.3656	49/64	19.4469	4	101.500	43	1092.20
3/16	4.7625	25/32	19.8437			44	1117.60
13/64	5.1594	51/64	20.2406	5	127.000	45	1143.00
7/32	5.5562	13/16	20.6375	6	152.400	46	1158.40
15/64	5.9531	53/64	21.0344	7	177.800	47	1193.80
1/4	6.3500	27/32	21.4312	8	203.200	48 (4ft)	1219.20
		55/64	21.8281	9	228.600		
17/64	6.7469	7/8	22.2250	10	254.001	49	1244.60
9/32	7.1437			11	279.401	50	1270.00
19/64	7.5406	57/64	22.6219	12 (1ft)	304.801	51	1295.40
5/16	7.9375	29/32	23.0187			52	1320.80
21/64	8.3344	59/64	23.4156	13	330.201	53	1346.20
11/32	8.7312	15/16	23.8125	14	355.601	54	1371.60
23/64	9.1281	61/64	24.2094	15	381.001	55	1397.00
3/8	9.5250	31/32	24.6062	16	406.401	56	1422.20
		63/64	25.0031	17	431.801	57	1447.80
25/64	9.9219	1	25.4001	18	457.201	58	1473.20
13/32	10.3187			19	482.601	59	1498.60
27/64	10.7156	1 1/8	28.5751	20	508.001	60 (5ft)	1524.00
7/16	11.1125	1 1/4	31.7501	21	533.401		
29/64	11.5094	1 3/8	34.9251	22	558.801	61	1549.40
15/32	11.9062	1 1/2	38.1001	23	584.201	62	1574.80
31/64	12.3031	1 5/8	41.2751	24 (2ft)	609.601	63	1600.20
1/2	12.7000	1 3/4	44.4501			64	1625.60
		1 7/8	47.6251	25	635.001	65	1651.00
33/64	13.0969	2	50.8001	26	660.401	66	1676.40
17/32	13.4937			27	685.801	67	1701.80
35/64	13.8906	2 1/8	53.9751	28	711.201	68	1727.20
9/16	14.2875	2 1/4	57.1501	29	736.601	69	1752.60
37/64	14.6844	2 3/8	60.3251	30	762.002	70	1778.00
19/32	15.0812	2 1/2	63.5001	31	787.402	71	1803.40
39/64	15.4781	2 5/8	66.6751	32	812.802	72 (6ft)	1828.80

METRIC/IMPERIAL CONVERSION TABLE
millimetres to inches

mm	in	mm	in	mm	in	mm	in
1	0.03937	26	1.02362	60	2.36221	310	12.2047
2	0.07874	27	1.06299	70	2.75591	320	12.5984
3	0.11811	28	1.10236	80	3.14961	330	12.9921
4	0.15748	29	1.14173	90	3.54331	340	13.3858
5	0.19685	30	1.18110	100	3.93701	350	13.7795
6	0.23622					360	14.1732
7	0.27559	31	1.22047	110	4.33071	370	14.5669
8	0.31496	32	1.25984	120	4.72441	380	14.9606
9	0.35433	33	1.29921	130	5.11811	390	15.3543
10	0.39370	34	1.33858	140	5.51181	400	15.7480
		35	1.37795	150	5.90552		
11	0.43307	36	1.41732	160	6.29922	410	16.1417
12	0.47244	37	1.45669	170	6.69292	420	16.5354
13	0.51181	38	1.49606	180	7.08662	430	16.9291
14	0.55118	39	1.53543	190	7.48032	440	17.3228
15	0.59055	40	1.57480	200	7.87402	450	17.7165
16	0.62992					460	18.1103
17	0.66929	41	1.61417	210	8.26772	470	18.5040
18	0.70866	42	1.65354	220	8.66142	480	18.8977
19	0.74803	43	1.69291	230	9.05513	490	19.2914
20	0.78740	44	1.73228	240	9.44883	500	19.6851
		45	1.77165	250	9.84252		
21	0.82677	46	1.81103	260	10.2362	600	23.6221
22	0.86614	47	1.85040	270	10.6299	700	27.5591
23	0.90551	48	1.88977	280	11.0236	800	31.4961
24	0.94488	49	1.92914	290	11.4173	900	35.4331
25	0.98425	50	1.96851	300	11.8110	1000	39.3701

SUPPLIERS

UK

ARNOLD LAVER TIMBERWORLD
Bramall Lane, Sheffield S2 4RJ, UK
Tel: 01142 556161
www.timberworld.co.uk
Timber, sheet materials or ancillary products

AXMINSTER POWER TOOL CENTRE
Chard Street, Axminster, Devon EX13 5DZ, UK
Tel: 0800 371822
www.axminster.co.uk
Extensive range of tools, machinery, accessories and
consumables

BARFORDS AQUACOTE
Alan Barford, 17 Ardley Works, London Road
Billericay CM12 9HP, UK
Tel: 01277 622050
www.barfords.com
Aquacote acrylic varnish

CLARKE INTERNATIONAL
Hemnal Street, Epping, Essex CM16 4LG, UK
Tel: 01992 565300
www.clarkeinternational.com
Major supplier and manufacturer of woodworking
hand and power tools

DEWALT POWER TOOLS
210 Bath Road, Slough, Berkshire SL1 3XE, UK
Tel: 01753 567055
www.dewalt.co.uk
Wide range of high-performance portable electric power
tools and accessories

ELEKTRA BECKUM
25 Majestic Road, Nursling Industrial Estate
Southampton, Hampshire SO16 0YT, UK
Tel: 02380 732000
www.electrabeckum.co.uk
Machinery, compressors and pneumatic tools

J. A. MILTON
Whitchurch Business Park, Whitchurch
Shropshire SY13 1LJ, UK
Tel: 01948 663434
www.jamiltonupholstery.co.uk
Upholstery materials and advice

BOSCH
Robert Bosch Power Tools
PO Box 98, Uxbridge UB9 5HN, UK
www.boschpowertools.co.uk
Power tools and accessories

LE PREVO LEATHERS
Dept W1, No.1 Charlotte Square
Newcastle upon Tyne NE1 4XF, UK
Tel: 0191 232 4179
www.leprevo.co.uk
Leather supplies

RYDENOR PRODUCTS
Units D and E, Dalton Airfield Industrial Estate
Dalton, Thirsk, North Yorkshire YO7 3HE, UK
Tel: 01845 578080
www.rydenor.co.uk
Materials, adhesives, abrasives, safety gear and
finishing products

SCREWFIX DIRECT
FREEPOST (within UK only), Yeovil
Somerset BA22 8BF, UK
Tel: 0500 414141
www.screwfix.com
Online supplier of trade tools, hardware products
and materials

TANSELI LIMITED
Unit 11, Imperial Park Industrial Estate, Towerfield Road
Shoeburyness, Essex SS3 9QT, UK
Tel: 01702 296888
www.tanseli.com
Tanseli wafers

TREND ROUTING TECHNOLOGY
Odhams Trading Estate, St Albans Road
Watford WD24 7TR, UK
Tel: 01923 224681
www.trendmachinery.co.uk

NORTH AMERICA

BOSCH
Robert Bosch, Postfach 106050
D-70049 Stuttgart, Germany
Tel: +49-711-8110
www.boschusa.com
Power tools and accessories

CLARKE POWER TOOLS INC.
28740 Glenwood Road, Perrysburg
Ohio 43551, USA
Tel: 800-2279603
www.clarkeusa.com
Major supplier and manufacturer of woodworking hand
and power tools

CMT USA INC.
307-F Pomona Drive
Greensboro NC 27407, USA
Tel: 336-854-0201
www.cmtusa.com
Router bits and accessories

DEWALT (CUSTOMER SERVICE)
626 Hanover Pike
Hampstead MD 21074, USA
Tel: 1-800-339258
www.dewalt.com
Wide range of high-performance portable electric power
tools and accessories

HITACHI POWER TOOLS
3950 Steve Reynolds Blvd
Norcross GA 30093, USA
Tel: 800-829-4752
www.hitachi.com
Compressors, generators and industrial machinery

JESADA TOOLS
310 Mears Boulevard
Oldsmar FL 34677 3047, USA
Tel: 813-891-6160
www. jesada.com
Router bits and accessories

MAKITA USA INC.
14930 Northam Street
La Mirada CA 90638, USA
Tel: 714-522-8088
www.makita.com
Power tools

METABO USA
Metabo Corporation
P.O. Box 2287, 1231 Wilson Drive
West Chester PA 19380, USA
Tel: 800-638-2264 `
www.metabousa.com
Power tools

TREND ROUTING TECHNOLOGY INC.
438 Foxhunt Drive
Walton, Kentucky KY 41094, USA
Tel: 859-485-2080
www.trend-usa.com
Routers and accessories

FURTHER INFORMATION

Charlesworth, David, *David Charlesworth's Furniture-making Techniques* (Lewes: GMC Publications, 1999)

Charlesworth, David, *David Charlesworth's Furniture-making Techniques* – Volume 2 (Lewes: GMC Publications, 2001)

Joyce, Ernest, *The Technique of Furniture Making*, Fourth Edition (London: Batsford, 1987; revised by Alan Peters)

Ley, Kevin, *Furniture Projects with the Router* (Lewes: GMC Publications, 2002)

Moser, Thomas, *How to Build Shaker Furniture*, Revised Edition (New York: Sterling, 1980)

Peters, Alan, *Cabinetmaking – The Professional Approach* (London: Stobart, 1984)

www.photobox.co.uk/kevinley@btopenworld.com
Kevin Ley's photography album website, featuring images of his furniture pieces.

www.linemine.com
Furniture plans are available to purchase online from *Furniture and Cabinetmaking* magazine's illustrator, Simon Rodway.

ABOUT THE AUTHOR

Kevin Ley retired from the Royal Air Force in 1987 and developed his hobby of funiture making into a successful business, designing and making bespoke pieces. He has been writing for GMC Publications for several years and now lives with his artist and teacher wife, Yvonne in their picturesque cottage in a wooded nature reserve.

Kevin divides his time between making furniture in his workshop next to the house, writing and photography for the GMC woodworking magazines, working with Yvonne on the improvements to their cottage, and maintenance of their large garden. Both enjoy fast cars, reading, talking, music, sampling the delights of the local eating and watering holes, keeping fit, and being in charge.

ACKNOWLEDGEMENTS

My thanks to all the staff at GMC Publications for their help along the rutted road of writing. To Paul Richardson for getting me started and his advice and patience, and April McCroskie for commissioning the book.

Also to Colin Eden-Eadon for his help and advice in publishing the original articles, to Mark Baker for the organization, to Gerrie Purcell for overseeing the project, Olivia Underhill for editing it, Jo Patterson for doing such a terrific job on the design, and of course to Jill Edwards and Janet Mitchell for their cheerful greetings on the phone. They are all a real pleasure to work with.

My greatest thanks though are to my wife Yvonne for her encouragement and helpful criticism, contributions to designs, assistance with the photography, and patience with the sawdust!

INDEX

Page numbers in bold refer to illustrations